Rejoicing in Our Hope

BISHOP ROBERT J. BAKER, S.T.D.

REJOICING
IN
OUR HOPE

Meditations *for the* Advent
and Christmas Seasons

EWTN PUBLISHING, INC.
IRONDALE, ALABAMA

Dedication

To all the Marchers for Life, hundreds of thousands of people, especially young people, who sought the overturn of *Roe v. Wade* and kept on marching, year after year, never losing hope—and to the courageous Supreme Court justices who voted to overrule *Roe v. Wade* (1973) and *Planned Parenthood v. Casey* (1992) in the landmark *Dobbs v. Jackson Women's Health Organization* decision (2022) and faced acrimony, harassment, and threats to their lives and well-being for the cause of Life.

We have such need in these times that can appear dark, in which we sometimes feel disoriented by the evil and violence that surround us, and by the distress of so many of our brothers and sisters. We need hope. We feel disoriented and rather discouraged because we are powerless, and it seems this darkness will never end.

We must not let hope abandon us, because God, with His love, walks with us.

I hope, because God is beside me.... I have hope, because God walks with me.

—Pope Francis

To come to know God—the true God—means to receive hope.

—Pope Benedict XVI

Rejoice in hope, be patient under trial, persevere in prayer.

—Romans 12:12

Contents

MEDITATIONS FOR THE CHRISTMAS SEASON

Acknowledgments

Most of these meditations appeared several years ago in the seasons of Advent and Christmas on EWTN. I am grateful to the staff of EWTN for helping those seasons be hope-filled with their televising those meditations. Our Sunday Visitor Press made available to their subscribers the Advent meditations contained here, originally broadcast on EWTN, and has given permission to EWTN to publish the main body of the meditations and the questions for reflection they added. I thank them for that kind gesture. Maria Kaczperski and Mary Dillard graciously provided many of the images found in these pages.

I am also grateful to Devin Jones and Taylor Wilson of EWTN Publishing for seeing value in their carrying these messages of hope through the medium of print in a broader way so that many more people can experience a joyful message of hope in the Advent and Christmas seasons!

Introduction

Accompanying you on your journey through the Advent and Christmas seasons will be daily meditations and prayers that aim at deepening your hope and joy. In the process, the Christian meaning of those two virtues will be partially unraveled. Their true meaning is always tied to our relationship with God—Father, Son, and Holy Spirit—as God is the giver of all gifts and graces. We rejoice in hope because God is on the horizon, and more precisely, because God is in our midst. God is with us in Jesus. Advent and Christmas are the seasons when we celebrate that reality in a unique and special way.

With the help of Advent candles and a Christ candle of hope, we will embrace the God of hope and joy in these holy seasons. Symbols are persons, places, events, or realities that in some way relate us to other persons, places, events, or realities. Religious symbols relate us to God. Candles are special religious symbols that remind us that Christ is the light of the world. We, as followers of Christ, are called to bring Christ's light into the world in which we live. A candle was presented to our godparents at the time of our Baptism. A candle will be a special symbol used at the Easter Vigil ceremony. One day, a candle will be placed in front of our casket at our Mass of Christian burial. In every situation, that candle is a symbol of Jesus Christ.

You will be invited each day of Advent to light an Advent candle as you pray the prayer at the end of the daily meditation. In the Christmas season, a large white candle that may have been placed in the middle of an Advent wreath, with its four candles for the four weeks of Advent, may be lit each day of the Christmas season, which extends from Christmas Day to the feast of the Baptism of the Lord, a movable feast. (Additional meditations are given to accommodate the changing times for the feast of the Baptism of the Lord.)

There can be different settings for these meditations and candle-lightings: a church, a chapel, a hall, or a home. Children might be asked to pray the daily prayer and light the candle.

May all who meditate on these messages, pray these prayers, and light these candles be led to the source of all our hope and joy, our Messiah, Lord, and Savior, Jesus Christ, the Son of God, born of the Blessed Virgin Mary in Bethlehem!

MEDITATIONS FOR THE ADVENT SEASON

We are waiting for the fulfillment of a promise. You will one day possess all this because God, as God, is Himself reality, realness, and intimacy.... Those who genuinely wait on the Lord God will not be disappointed. They will grow into this true meeting with God, an encounter in mystery and grace. It all depends upon our waiting, staying vigilant, and straining toward what lies ahead with true openness.

Advent is a time of being deeply shaken, so that man will wake up to himself. The prerequisite for a fulfilled Advent is a renunciation of the arrogant gestures and tempting dreams with which, and in which man is always deceiving himself.[1]

— Fr. Alfred Delp, S.J.

[1] From Advent prison meditations written by Father Alfred Delp, S.J., who was executed for treason for his opposition to Hitler's government. His allusion to "arrogant gestures and tempting dreams with which ... man is always deceiving himself" probably is, at least partly, a veiled allusion to the Nazi regime.

Week 1

Day 1

Advent: A Season of Hope

The Church centers its attention these days on a season we call Advent, a season of preparation and hope. We are summoned in the first week of Advent to be on guard, to be ready and prepared for the coming of the Lord.

Unfortunately, this holy season gets lost in the shuffle of preparations for Christmas already begun in our secular society. There is a maze of glitter and frivolity that highlights the material aspects of a feast that is long off and misses the true spiritual meaning of that event.

So we need the Advent season to help us focus our attention on the spiritual preparation for the celebration of this greatest event of history, the birth of Christ. All too quickly Christmas Day will be here. It will have much more meaning for us if we have prepared for that day spiritually.

I invite you to take out a moment each day to reflect with me as we "rejoice in hope" (Rom. 12:12) this Advent season, with our spiritual guides being the psalmist, the writers of other books of Sacred Scripture, various saints, theologians, and authors, and recent popes.

Take out a little time to enter into the season with hope in your heart, awaiting this coming feast as the people of Israel did, as Simeon and Anna did, as John the Baptist did, as Joseph and Mary did.

You will find, as they did, that God comes in a special way to the people who steadfastly hope for His coming.

For Reflection, Action, or Commitment

How did I celebrate Advent in the past?
How will celebrate this Advent?

Light a Candle

Let us pray: "Lord, watch over Your people, who come to You in confidence; strengthen the hearts of those who hope in You. Give courage to those who falter because of their failures. Lead them along in this holy season of Advent closer to You in hope by the power of Your Holy Spirit. May they one day proclaim Your saving acts of kindness in Your eternal Kingdom. Amen."

Day 2

The Meaning of Hope

My dear friends, we continue our meditations for the Advent season—"rejoicing in hope."

Hope is a virtue that is critical for survival in life. We won't last long without it. We die physically, emotionally, and spiritually without it. Living involves hoping.

The *Catechism of the Catholic Church* (1817) says that "hope is the theological virtue by which we desire the kingdom of heaven and eternal life as our happiness,... relying not on our strength, but on the help of the grace of the Holy Spirit." The *Catechism* tells us that "Christian hope takes up and fulfills the hope of the chosen people which has its origin and model in the hope of Abraham, who was blessed abundantly by the promises of God fulfilled in Isaac, and who was purified by the test of the sacrifice. 'Hoping against hope, he believed, and thus became the father of many nations'" (CCC 1819).

The people of Israel, then, starting with Abraham, were a "people of hope." It is good for us in the Advent season to pick up the great Jewish book of prayer that is the Psalms and meditate on the messages of hope that are found there.

I can assure you, there are many.

Take, for example, the words of Psalm 131 verses 2 and 3: "Rather, I have stilled my soul, Like a weaned child to its mother, weaned is my soul. Israel, hope in the Lord, now and forever."

Can you imagine anyone more at peace than an infant in its mother's arms? The psalmist tells us that we should be just as much at peace with the Lord, Who is like a caring mother. "O Israel, hope in the Lord, both now and forever," because you bring us peace.

For Reflection, Action, or Commitment

What meaning do I give to the word hope?

Light a Candle

Let us pray: "Lord, watch over Your people, who come to You in confidence. Strengthen the hearts of those who hope in You. Give courage to those who falter because of their failures. Lead them along in this holy season of Advent closer to You in hope by the power of Your Holy Spirit. May they one day proclaim Your saving acts of kindness in Your eternal Kingdom. Amen."

Day 3

A Fireside Chat on Hope

In the midst of the Great Depression of the 1930s, the American president at the time, Franklin Delano Roosevelt, told a struggling nation during his March 4, 1933, inaugural address: "All we have to fear is fear itself.... This great nation will endure, as it has endured, will revive and will prosper."

The tone of his message was a confident one for a people who, at the time, lacked confidence and hope, a people fearing not only for the future but even for the present. How would they put food on the table for their families when they were out of work? Nearly all businesses in the country were struggling. Few banks in the country were open for normal business activity. The economy was at a standstill. Despair was in the air.

Roosevelt conducted regular "fireside chats" with the nation, which succeeded in bringing the president closer to the people and helping them through a terrible crisis, giving them hope.

The psalmist had a similar optimism in the face of impending war. In Psalm 27, he reminds the people that the Lord is their light and salvation. Whom should they fear?

"The Lord is my life's refuge; of whom should I be afraid?... Though an army encamp against me, my heart does not fear;

Though war be waged against me, even then do I trust" (Ps. 27:1, 3).

And Psalm 56 takes up the same theme: "when I am afraid, in you I place my trust. I praise the word of God; I trust in God, I do not fear. What can mere flesh do to me?... This I know: God is on my side" (vv. 4-5, 10).

"This I know: God is on my side" (v. 10). Would that we had the kind of hope the psalmist had! He conveys that hope to all those who pick up his words and find consolation and strength from them. Hope revives for those who put their trust in God, no matter what.

For Reflection, Action, or Commitment

How do I face the fears I have?

Light a Candle

Let us pray: "Lord, watch over Your people, who come to You in confidence. Strengthen the hearts of those who hope in You. Give courage to those who falter because of their failures. Lead them along in this holy season of Advent closer to You in hope by the power of Your Holy Spirit. May they one day proclaim Your saving acts of kindness in Your eternal Kingdom. Amen."

Day 4

If God Is for Us ...

Overlooking the northern outer belt around Columbus, Ohio, Interstate 270, is an imposing steeple on the top of the Josephi-num seminary on North High St. I attended that seminary back in the 1960s. It was originally founded to send German-speaking priests to German immigrants in the late nineteenth and early twentieth centuries.

On the cornerstone of that magnificent edifice are the Latin words of St. Paul to the Romans: "*Si Deus Pro nobis, quis contra nos?*" (If God is for us, who can be against us?).

This powerful message of St. Paul is found in his great treatise on hope in chapter 8 of his Letter to the Romans, beginning with verse 24: "In hope we were saved." Pope Benedict XVI was so captivated by those words that he began his wonderful encyclical *Spe Salvi* with them.

St. Paul writes so eloquently:

In hope we were saved. But hope is not hope if its object is seen; how is it possible for one to hope for what he sees? And hoping for what we cannot see means awaiting it with patient endurance.... We know that God makes all things work together for the good of those who love him who have been called according to his decree.... If God is for us, who can be against us? (Rom. 8:24-25, 28, 31)

St. Paul prefaces these comments with a realistic assessment of the human condition: "Creation," he says, "was made subject to futility, not of its own accord but by him who once subjected it; yet not without hope, because the world itself will be freed from its slavery to corruption and share in the glorious freedom of the children of God" (Rom. 8:20-21).

Despite all the mess in the world caused by the sin of Adam and our own selfishness and sinfulness, God has not given up on us. Or so says St. Paul. *"Si Deus Pro nobis, quis contra nos?"* (If God is for us, who can be against us?). And "in hope," he says, we have been saved. Thanks be to God!

For Reflection, Action, or Commitment

Do I have a sense that God is so strong a force that nothing can undermine His power in my life if I do His holy will?

Light a Candle

Let us pray: "Lord, watch over Your people, who come to You in confidence. Strengthen the hearts of those who hope in You. Give courage to those who falter because of their failures. Lead them along in this holy season of Advent closer to You in hope by the power of Your Holy Spirit. May they one day proclaim Your saving acts of kindness in Your eternal Kingdom. Amen."

Day 5

The One Who Hopes
Lives Differently

The psalmist sums up his reason for hope: "When I am afraid, in you I place my trust. I praise the word of God; . . . This I know: God is on my side" (Ps. 56:4–5, 10).

There you have it! The person who believes and trusts in God has it all over the person who doesn't connect to a personal God!

Pope Benedict XVI, in his encyclical *Spe Salvi*, says the same: "To come to know God — the true God — means to receive hope."[2] "The dark door of time, of the future, has been thrown open, the one who has hope lives differently; the one who hopes has been granted the gift of a new life."[3]

I've seen that difference; you have too — in people with hope. I think of my sister-in-law, Arlene, who was told she had ovarian cancer. It was a devastating piece of information to digest. I went to visit her with the Sacrament of the Anointing of the Sick. I told her that was Jesus coming to her in the Sacrament. He was at her

---

[2] Benedict XVI, Encyclical Letter *Spe Salvi* (November 30, 2007), no. 3.

[3] Ibid., no. 2.

15

bedside. Shortly afterward, she began to perk up. Her attitude, her spirits changed; she had a new lease on life.

She was able to get back to daily Mass, as she had before. And her words to me later on were: "I don't know whether I should be praying for a cure. So many blessings have come to me through this illness." Arlene had been a constant source of inspiration to hundreds of people since, including her own husband, my brother, also diagnosed with cancer.

Arlene lived the gospel of hope, she preached it with her life. She didn't go around sullen or despondent. She had a positive attitude, no matter what the situation, the way all who trust in the Lord should have. Eventually, the Lord called her to be with Him. But in her illness, she never lost hope.

"This I know: God is on my side" (Ps. 56:10). "When I am afraid, in you I place my trust. I praise the word of God" (Ps. 56:4–5).

For Reflection, Action, or Commitment

Do I live differently because I have hope?

Light a Candle

Let us pray: "Lord, watch over Your people, who come to You in confidence. Strengthen the hearts of those who hope in You. Give courage to those who falter because of their failures. Lead them along in this holy season of Advent closer to You in hope by the power of Your Holy Spirit. May they one day proclaim Your saving acts of kindness in Your eternal Kingdom. Amen."

Day 6

Hope and the Future

St. Paul, in his letter to the Philippians, indicates that he has not yet reached the goal he is aspiring to. He has not yet finished the course, grasped the prize, or reached the finish line.

"It is not that I have reached it yet, or have already finished my course, but I am racing to grasp the prize, if possible.... Brothers, I do not think of myself as having reached the finish line. I give no thought to what lies behind, but push on to what is ahead. My entire attention is on the finish line" (Phil. 3:12-14).

Pope Benedict says much the same in his encyclical *Spe Salvi*: "In hope we were saved." A distinguishing mark of Christians, he says, is the fact that they have a future: "It is not that they know the details of what awaits them, but they know in general terms that their life will not end in emptiness. Only when the future is certain as a positive reality does it become possible to live the present as well," says the pope.[4]

The poet Robert Browning put it this way: "A man's reach should exceed his grasp, or what's a heaven for?"

---

[4] Benedict XVI, Encyclical Letter *Spe Salvi* (November 30, 2007), no. 2.

Hope is a future-oriented virtue. It acknowledges that there is a future awaiting us that is much, much better than the present. The virtue of hope, with its orientation to the future, enables us to handle present distresses and struggles in a positive way.

The letter to the Hebrews, recalling the faith of the ancients, says of them, "All of these died in faith. They did not obtain what had been promised but saw and saluted it from afar. By acknowledging themselves to be strangers and foreigners on the earth, they showed that they were seeking a homeland. If they had been thinking back to the place from which they had come, they would have had the opportunity of returning there. But they were searching for a better, heavenly home. Wherefore God is not ashamed to be called their God, for He has prepared a city for them" (11:13–16).

Pope Benedict reminds us that this perspective does not mean for one moment that we live only for the future.[5] People in hope are building up the kingdom on earth, but they are also on pilgrimage to that eternal Kingdom God has in store for those who follow Him.

For Reflection, Action, or Commitment

What did Robert Browning mean when he wrote, "a man's reach should exceed his grasp, or what's a heaven for?"

[5] See ibid., no. 4.

Light a Candle

Let us pray: "Lord, watch over Your people, who come to You in confidence. Strengthen the hearts of those who hope in You. Give courage to those who falter because of their failures. Lead them along in this holy season of Advent closer to You in hope by the power of Your Holy Spirit. May they one day proclaim Your saving acts of kindness in Your eternal Kingdom. Amen."

Day 7

After This, Our Exile

Fr. Benedict Groeschel, now deceased, has some wonderful meditations on hope in his book *After This Life*. In fact, the whole book is about hope. It presents a realistic portrayal of life in the present in expectation of life hereafter. He says he first thought of giving the book the title "After This Our Exile" and cites the reference of Blessed Herman of Richenau, a thousand years ago, in his beautiful prayer to Our Lady, the *Salve Regina*: "After this, our exile, show unto us the blessed fruit of thy womb, Jesus."

Fr. Groeschel explains why Blessed Herman used the word *exile* for this life. The monk who wrote these words was blind and crippled. His disabilities, says Fr. Groeschel "led him to see more clearly than most that his life was an exile from his real home with our Heavenly Father, Christ, the Virgin Mary, and the saints.... The only thing that kept him going was the certitude that the life he was living was not the only thing that God had in store for him—that his exile was temporary, and he would one day go home."[6]

---

[6] Benedict J. Groeschel, *After This Life: What Catholics Believe about What Happens Next* (Huntington, IN: Our Sunday Visitor, 2009), 16-17.

This is a valid perspective on hope: this life is, in a real sense, an exile; Heaven is our real home.

Fr. Groeschel says that, at times, he feels the same way. "The effects of my accident of several years ago still linger," he says, "making many tasks that once were simple very difficult."

Additionally, he suffered a small stroke, making him aware of "new and annoying limitations." He prayed the *Salve Regina* often, and it helped him to recall that his present life, his exile from God, "is temporary, a mere prelude to a life more wonderful and more vibrant than any of us can imagine."

He said, "This life on earth can have moments of exquisite beauty, of great satisfaction, but it can also be a 'valley of tears.' . . . A vital awareness of the promise of the life to come, the life that the Son of God won for us by his holy life, terrible death, and glorious resurrection fills us with hope and strength in facing this life and its inevitable challenges — in looking forward with courage and in hope to what comes next."[7] Thank you, Fr. Groeschel, for those marvelous insights!

For Reflection, Action, or Commitment

How does seeing this life as a "prelude to a life more wonderful and more vibrant" give us hope?

[7] Ibid., 17.

Light a Candle

Let us pray: "Lord, watch over Your people, who come to You in confidence. Strengthen the hearts of those who hope in You. Give courage to those who falter because of their failures. Lead them along in this holy season of Advent closer to You in hope by the power of Your Holy Spirit. May they one day proclaim Your saving acts of kindness in Your eternal Kingdom. Amen."

Week 2

Day 8

Life Eternal: A Possibility beyond All Human Life

As we continue our meditations on hope in this season of Advent, I once again borrow an insight from Fr. Benedict Groeschel's beautiful book *After This Life*.

This insightful teacher, preacher, and writer alludes to words Christ spoke to His followers at the Last Supper, beginning with the words "let not your hearts be troubled; believe in God, believe also in me. In my Father's house are many rooms; if it were not so, would I have told you that I go to prepare a place for you? And when I go and prepare a place for you, I will come again and will take you to myself, that where I am you may be also" (1 John 14:1–7).

Heartening words from our Savior that are "simultaneously the promise of eternal joy in our heavenly father's home and the preparation for the horrible torture and life-giving death of his Son."[8] "As we meditate on these words," says Fr. Groeschel, "we discover ourselves immersed in horror and death, in failure and desolation — it is as if we are drowning. But we find we are soon brought with Christ out of the depths to everlasting hope and to

8 Groeschel, *After This Life*, 83.

something almost too exalted for us to imagine: life eternal for sinful man."

"Life eternal: this is a thought beyond the comprehension of creatures who live in our dying world. It is a possibility beyond all human hope, and it is offered to us despite the fact that even the best of us—the great saints among us—can never be worthy of it."

St. Paul addresses the Colossians with a similar message of hope, as he tells them, "We always give thanks to God, the Father of our Lord Jesus Christ, when we pray for you, for we have heard of your faith in Christ Jesus and the love that you have for all the holy ones because of the hope reserved for you in heaven. Of this you have already heard through the word of truth, the gospel, that has come to you. Just as in the whole world it is bearing fruit and growing, so also among you" (Col. 1:3-6).

For Reflection, Action, or Commitment

Why should we not "let our hearts be troubled"?

Light a Candle

Let us pray: "Lord, watch over Your people, who come to You in confidence. Strengthen the hearts of those who hope in You. Give courage to those who falter because of their failures. Lead them along in this holy season of Advent closer to You in hope by the power of Your Holy Spirit. May they one day proclaim Your saving acts of kindness in Your eternal Kingdom. Amen."

Day 9

Earthly Responsibilities and Hope

The Pastoral Constitution on the Church in the Modern World of the Second Vatican Council, *Gaudium et Spes*, pointed out that "the joys and hopes, the grief and anguish of the people of our time, especially of those who are poor or afflicted, are the joys and hopes, the grief and anguish of the followers of Christ as well. Nothing that is genuinely human fails to find an echo in their hearts." The council fathers went on to say in that 1965 document that "it is a mistake to think that because we have here no lasting city, but seek the city which is to come, we are entitled to evade our earthly responsibilities; this is to forget that because of our faith we are all the more bound to fulfil these responsibilities according to each one's vocation."[9]

In Matthew's Gospel, we discover the judgment scene depicted as the Son of Man enthroned with His angels summoning all the nations of the world and separating them, one from another as a shepherd separates sheep from goats. Those who inherit the kingdom will be those who fed the hungry, gave drink to the thirsty,

---

[9]   Vatican Council II, Pastoral Constitution on the Church in the Modern World *Gaudium et Spes* (December 7, 1965), no. 43.

clothed the naked, welcomed the stranger, and visited the sick and imprisoned. In other words, those who unknowingly helped the Lord Himself in helping others (see Matt. 25:31-46).

In his encyclical *Spe Salvi*, Pope Benedict XVI reminds us that "from the earliest times, the prospect of the judgment has influenced Christians in their daily living as a criterion by which to order their present life, as a summons to their conscience, and at the same time as hope in God's justice.... This looking ahead has given Christianity its importance for the present moment."[10] "Faith in the Last Judgment is first and foremost hope—the need for which was made abundantly clear in the upheavals of recent centuries."[11] The pope is convinced that "the question of justice constitutes the essential argument, or in any case, the strongest argument, in favor of faith in eternal life."[12] Our actions with God and others in this life will determine our union with God and others in eternal life. That is our great hope.

For Reflection, Action, or Commitment

Why are our actions with God and others in this life important?

---

[10] Benedict XVI, Encyclical Letter *Spe Salvi* (November 30, 2007), no. 40.
[11] Ibid., no. 43.
[12] Ibid., no. 40.

Light a Candle

Let us pray: "Lord, watch over Your people, who come to You in confidence. Strengthen the hearts of those who hope in You. Give courage to those who falter because of their failures. Lead them along in this holy season of Advent closer to You in hope by the power of Your Holy Spirit. May they one day proclaim Your saving acts of kindness in Your eternal Kingdom. Amen."

Day 10

Putting Off Heaven

A priest celebrating holy Mass for students of a Catholic elementary school asked the question in his homily: "Who wants to be a saint and be with Jesus in Heaven?" Everyone raised their hands and waved them, all but one small youngster sitting close to the priest. The priest barely got the words out "Why not?" when the young boy, by the name of Raymond, explained, "I want to be a saint, but as for going to Heaven now, I'm too young to die." Raymond was just ten years old. Raymond was sincere in his answer, based on how he understood Heaven.

Heaven is a mystery. Great saints, such as St. Thomas, have homed in on some of its characteristics. The *Catechism of the Catholic Church* states that "Heaven is the ultimate end and fulfillment of the deepest human longings, the state of supreme, definitive happiness" (1024). It is "eternal life with God; communion of life and love with the Trinity and all the blessed" (glossary).

If we really understood its meaning at the level of the heart, we would all long for Heaven, not want to avoid it. Most of us are probably closer to young Raymond in our desire to put off Heaven till a later date. To that extent, we are lacking in the virtue of hope.

I think of people stricken with seemingly incurable diseases at an early age, like Cindy, the mother of three, who at thirty-one was diagnosed with an aggressive form of lymphoma shortly after giving birth to her third child. A tumor the size of a brick had invisibly laid claim to her body and was perched right over her unborn son. Little Brandon was born several weeks before he was due. Cindy's cancer eventually went into remission, but the lifesaving treatments for cancer severely damaged her heart and lungs. Hope did not come easy for her at first, but with the strength God gives her in prayer, she now discovers that she is not alone. She is able to welcome God's help in support of her dear family members, including Brandon, who is now almost seven years old. God is helping her face whatever the future brings, in hope. May He do the same for us!

For Reflection, Action, or Commitment

What age is too young to be called to eternal life?

Light a Candle

Let us pray: "Lord, watch over Your people, who come to You in confidence. Strengthen the hearts of those who hope in You. Give courage to those who falter because of their failures. Lead them along in this holy season of Advent closer to You in hope by the power of Your Holy Spirit. May they one day proclaim Your saving acts of kindness in Your eternal Kingdom. Amen."

Day 11

Prayer and Hope

Prayer does make a difference when it comes to hope.

The psalmist says as much: "You are my hope, Lord; my trust, God, from my youth.... On you I have depended since birth," he says. "I will always hope in you and add to all your praise" (Ps. 71:5, 6, 14).

Psalm 33 assures us that "the eye of the Lord is upon those who fear him, upon those who count on his mercy, To deliver their soul from death, and to keep them alive through famine" (vv. 18–19).

Sam Ceccola would attest to that fact. Eighteen years ago, he first beat lymphoma. Then he beat skin cancer, brain cancer, lung cancer, and prostate cancer. And he's still fighting and praying. What scared him was not the idea of death, as he'd come to deal with that possibility when his cancer first appeared in 1992. What scared him was, rather, concern for his wife, who was waging her own private battle with fibromyalgia. Sam made up his mind to do everything he still could to make life easier for her.[13]

Besides mantle cell lymphoma, a rare and often lethal form of cancer, he also fought into remission prostate and lung cancer and

[13] See *Spirit*, September 2010, 92–96.

faced surgery to remove a malignant brain tumor. Sam's oncologist would have given him a 1-in-10 chance of survival. Radiation treatments for the lymphoma burned up his salivary glands and damaged his jaw. He suffered several attacks of a rare pneumonia that inflamed his lungs. He was diagnosed with myelodysplastic syndrome, often a precursor to leukemia, and also had a recurrence of melanoma. He was fortunate when benign polyps were found in his bladder.

People ask him all the time for his secret. How does he keep going? He answers, "I can only pray that I've inherited some of my father's genes." His ninety-four-year-old father still lives on his own. Above all, he says he trusts God and his doctors. That sounds like a good prescription for anyone. Praying does make a difference. It helps us put our trust in God and other people, who care for us.

For Reflection, Action, or Commitment
Why do prayers make a difference?

Light a Candle

Let us pray: "Lord, watch over Your people, who come to You in confidence. Strengthen the hearts of those who hope in You. Give courage to those who falter because of their failures. Lead them along in this holy season of Advent closer to You in hope by the power of Your Holy Spirit. May they one day proclaim Your saving acts of kindness in Your eternal Kingdom. Amen."

Day 12

God Is Rich in Mercy

The diary of the great saint of Divine Mercy, St. Maria Faustina, contains reflections, prayers, and mystical insights of this saint, who received various private revelations from Our Lord regarding His Divine Mercy. These messages fulfill Our Lord's Gospel command to "be merciful as your father is merciful" (Luke 6:36) and how to receive the Lord's promise, "Blessed are the merciful for they shall obtain mercy" (Matt. 5:7).

Pope Saint John Paul II, in his encyclical *Dives in Misericordia* (Rich in Mercy), wrote that "the Church must consider it one of her principal duties — at every stage of history and especially in our modern age — to proclaim and to introduce into life the mystery of mercy, supremely revealed in Jesus Christ."[14] This pope beatified and canonized St. Maria Faustina and promoted her devotion by establishing Divine Mercy Sunday, the first Sunday after Easter.

Many churches display the portrait revealing the merciful Christ, with these words beneath the picture: "Jesus, I trust in You."

---

[14] John Paul II, Encyclical *Dives in Misericordia* (November 30, 1980), no. 14.

The Lord promised a great grace to St. Faustina and all those who will proclaim His Divine Mercy. He would protect them in the hour of death. "Even if the sins of souls will be as dark as night," he told St. Faustina.[15]

How important it is for people to look to the merciful Christ, seeking the grace of conversion, and entrusting themselves to His merciful compassion! The words "Jesus, I trust in You" have the power to lead one to the mercy Christ holds in store for all who seek His forgiveness and love. Those words may be the avenue to a good confession in the Sacrament of Reconciliation and to union with Christ in the Holy Eucharist. Let us follow St. Faustina's lead and express our trust in the Lord's fathomless mercy!

For Reflection, Action, or Commitment

How can I lead someone to the mercy of Christ?

Light a Candle

Let us pray: "Lord, watch over Your people, who come to You in confidence. Strengthen the hearts of those who hope in You. Give courage to those who falter because of their failures. Lead them along in this holy season of Advent closer to You in hope by the power of Your Holy Spirit. May they one day proclaim Your saving acts of kindness in Your eternal Kingdom. Amen."

---

[15] Maria Faustina Kowalska, *Diary of Saint Maria Faustina Kowalska: Divine Mercy in My Soul* (Stockbridge, MA: Marian Press, 2014), no. 378.

Day 13

Appealing to the Mercy of Christ

The Lord granted special messages of hope in Divine Mercy to St. Maria Faustina, a Polish saint of the twentieth century. The Lord told her:

> Let the greatest sinners place their trust in my mercy. They have the right before others to trust in the abyss of my mercy. . . .
>
> I cannot punish even the greatest sinner if he makes an appeal to my compassion, but on the contrary, I justify him in my unfathomable and inscrutable mercy. . . . Before I come as a just judge, I first open wide the door of my mercy. He who refuses to pass through the door of my mercy must pass through the door of my justice.[16]

And the Lord told St. Faustina that He is "more generous toward sinners than toward the just. It was for their sake that I came down from heaven." He said, "It was for their sake that my

---

[16] Ibid., no. 1146.

blood was spilled. Let them not fear to approach me; they are most in need of my mercy."[17]

"Oh, if sinners knew my mercy, they would not perish in such great numbers. Tell sinful souls not to be afraid to approach me; speak to them of my great mercy."[18] "The loss of each soul plunges me into mortal sadness. You always console me when you pray for sinners. The prayer most pleasing to me is prayer for the conversion of sinners. Know, my daughter, that this prayer is always heard and answered."[19]

A great prayer during the Advent season would be a prayer of hope in Divine Mercy for the conversion of some person you know who is far away from God. That person may be yourself. Just utter these words, "Jesus, I trust in You," and He will not be far from you.

Our words today are the words of the psalmist: "But I trust in your mercy. Grant my heart joy in your salvation, I will sing to the Lord, for he has dealt bountifully with me" (Ps. 13:6). With St. Augustine we pray, "All my hope lies only in your great mercy."

For Reflection, Action, or Commitment

Offer a prayer for the conversion of someone far from the Lord.

---

[17] Ibid., no. 1275.
[18] Ibid., no. 1396.
[19] Ibid., no. 1397.

Light a Candle

Let us pray: "Lord, watch over Your people, who come to You in confidence. Strengthen the hearts of those who hope in You. Give courage to those who falter because of their failures. Lead them along in this holy season of Advent closer to You in hope by the power of Your Holy Spirit. May they one day proclaim Your saving acts of kindness in Your eternal Kingdom. Amen."

Day 14

Joy in Hope over the Sinner Who Repents

We continue our Advent meditations on hope, and we underline the most powerful reason for hope: the divine mercy of God toward all of us as sinners. The parables of the prodigal son, the lost coin, and the lost sheep of Luke's Gospel dramatically portray the mystery of divine mercy. There, we hear the Lord say, "There will be more joy in heaven over one sinner who repents than over ninety-nine righteous people who have no need of repentance" (Luke 15:7).

St. Paul's First Letter to Timothy describes Paul's remarkable conversion: "I was once a blasphemer and a persecutor and arrogant," he says, "but I have been mercifully treated because I acted out of ignorance in my unbelief. Indeed, the grace of Our Lord has been abundant, along with the faith and love that are Christ Jesus. This saying," he says, "is trustworthy and deserves full acceptance: Christ came into the world to save sinners. Of these I am the foremost. But for that reason I was mercifully treated, so that in me, as the foremost, Christ Jesus might display all his patience as an example for those who would come to believe in him for everlasting life" (1:12–17).

St. Maria Faustina, the saint of Divine Mercy, received these special words of hope in a private revelation from the Lord: "When a soul sees and realizes the gravity of its sins, when the whole abyss of the misery into which it immersed itself is displayed before its eyes, let it not despair; but with trust let it throw itself into the arms of my mercy, as a child into the arms of its beloved mother. These souls have a right of priority to my compassionate Heart; they have first access to my mercy. Tell them that no soul that has called upon my mercy has been disappointed or brought to shame. I delight particularly in a soul which has placed its trust in my goodness."[20]

What a powerful message of hope for us in this Advent season! No one is without hope who places his or her trust in the divine mercy of God. "Jesus, I trust in You!"

For Reflection, Action, or Commitment

Can I help someone I know hope in God's
mercy by some prayer or action?

Light a Candle

[20] Ibid., 1541.

Let us pray: "Lord, watch over Your people, who come to You in confidence. Strengthen the hearts of those who hope in You. Give courage to those who falter because of their failures. Lead them along in this holy season of Advent closer to You in hope by the power of Your Holy Spirit. May they one day proclaim Your saving acts of kindness in Your eternal Kingdom. Amen."

Week 3

Day 15

Joy and Hope

We light a rose-colored candle today on the third Sunday of Advent, a Sunday traditionally referred to as *Gaudete* Sunday. *Gaudete* is the Latin word for "rejoice," and it is the first word of the entrance antiphon for today's Mass, which contains words from St. Paul's letter to the Philippians: "Rejoice in the Lord always! I say it again. Rejoice!" (4:4). These words highlight our joyful expectation of the Lord's birth and second coming. Rose-colored vestments are permitted for Mass on this day as well.

Joy and hope are sister virtues. Hope spawns joy. The psalmist got it right when he prayed, "As for me, I trust in your merciful love. Let my heart rejoice in your saving help. Let me sing to the Lord for His goodness to me, singing psalms to the name of the Lord, the Most High" (Ps. 13:6).

"I trust in your merciful love. Let my heart rejoice in your saving help." It's time for us to pull out the stops and do a little rejoicing today. "Rejoice in the Lord always," St. Paul says. "I say it again. Rejoice!" I lifted another verse from St. Paul, connecting hope and joy, for the motto of my episcopal coat of arms. It is from Romans 12:12. There, St. Paul tells the Romans: "Rejoice in hope, be patient under trial, persevere in prayer."

"Rejoicing in Hope" is my motto, and sharing that message has been part of my time as a bishop. I have now spent fifty-three years as a priest and twenty-four years as a bishop. I have seen much transpire in the Church and in the world these past years. My role as a priest and bishop has been one of preaching hope to my people, giving them reasons for hope and joy.

Hope and joy come from the expectation of good things now and good things to come. And those good things come from the good news we preach. With St. Paul, I have come to see all good centered in God. All our hope is in Him. When we put our hope in passing values and fads, it quickly diminishes. It dies out. When God enters the picture, there is hope; there is joy. He is our reason for hope. He is our reason for joy. Gaudete! Rejoice! The Lord is near! The Lord is here.

For Reflection, Action, or Commitment

Do I inspire hope and joy in others? How can I do that better?

Light a Candle

Let us pray: "Lord, watch over Your people, who come to You in confidence. Strengthen the hearts of those who hope in You. Give courage to those who falter because of their failures. Lead them along in this holy season of Advent closer to You in hope by the power of Your Holy Spirit. May they one day proclaim Your saving acts of kindness in Your eternal Kingdom. Amen."

Day 16

What the World Needs Now: Hope

"The contemporary world above all needs hope," says Pope Benedict XVI.[21] He says that "developing peoples need it, but so do those who are economically advanced. We are becoming increasingly aware that we are all on one boat and together must save each other. Seeing so much false security collapse, we realize that what we need most is trustworthy hope. This is found," said Pope Benedict, "in Christ alone."

"If Jesus is present, there is no longer any time that lacks meaning or is empty. If He is present, we may continue to hope, even when others can no longer assure us of any support, even when the present becomes trying."[22]

Our single most important reason for hoping in the Advent season is the coming of Christ into our world, into our lives.

The word *Advent* itself can mean "coming," "arrival," or "presence." The ancient world used the word to indicate the arrival of an important official, a king, or an emperor. It could also mean the coming of the divinity in some way.

---

[21] Benedict XVI, Angelus Address (November 29, 2009).
[22] Ibid.

Pope Benedict said that Christians have used the word *Advent* to express "their relationship with Jesus Christ: Jesus is the king who entered this poor 'province' called 'earth' to pay everyone a visit; he makes all those who believe in him participate in his coming."[23]

For Christians, the essential meaning of the Latin word *adventus* was "God is here. He has not withdrawn from the world, he has not deserted us. Even if we cannot see and touch as we can tangible realities, he is here and comes to visit us."[24] His *adventus*, God's coming in Christ, is our most important reason for hope in this holy Advent season.

For Reflection, Action, or Commitment

Reflect on these words: "If Jesus is present, there is no longer any time that lacks meaning or hope."

Light a Candle

Let us pray: "Lord, watch over Your people, who come to You in confidence. Strengthen the hearts of those who hope in You. Give courage to those who falter because of their failures. Lead them along in this holy season of Advent closer to You in hope by the power of Your Holy Spirit. May they one day proclaim Your saving acts of kindness in Your eternal Kingdom. Amen."

[23] Benedict XVI, Homily (November 28, 2009).
[24] Ibid.

Day 17

Christ, the Basis of Hope

Pope Benedict XVI said that "hope marks humanity's journey, but for Christians it is enlivened by a certainty: The Lord is present in the passage of our lives. He accompanies us and will one day also dry our tears. One day, not far off, everything will find its fulfilment in the kingdom of God, a kingdom of justice and peace."[25]

Pope Benedict sees Christ as relevant not only to Christians, "or only to believers, but to all men and women, for Christ, who is the center of faith, is also the foundation of hope. And every human being is constantly in need of hope."[26]

From the pope's perspective, then, "every human being is constantly in need of hope," and "Christ is the center of faith and the foundation of hope."

Like you, like the pope, I can think of a million reasons why people are in need of hope. Read the front page of your daily newspaper, the police blotter, the editorial page, the obituary page; you name it, the reasons are there. People are besieged by wars, hunger, starvation, epidemics, genocide, tsunamis, hurricanes,

[25] Ibid.
[26] Benedict XVI, Angelus Address (November 29, 2009).

earthquakes, tornadoes, all suffering and distressed peoples, those forced to emigrate because of natural disasters, all the world's deceased—you name it.

Yet there is a single most important reason for hope that underlines all others: that is the advent, the coming, of Christ.

In this holy Advent season, we take time to meditate on this reason for our hope; we delve into its mystery and grandeur; we allow ourselves the spiritual opportunity to let this message penetrate our minds and hearts, leading us to hope and joy, leading us to help the coming of Christ make a difference in our lives and in the world in which we live.

For Reflection, Action, or Commitment

Think of reasons why people need hope.
How can Christ give them hope?

Light a Candle

Let us pray: "Lord, watch over Your people, who come to You in confidence. Strengthen the hearts of those who hope in You. Give courage to those who falter because of their failures. Lead them along in this holy season of Advent closer to You in hope by the power of Your Holy Spirit. May they one day proclaim Your saving acts of kindness in Your eternal Kingdom. Amen."

Day 18

How Christ Makes a Difference

When it comes to living a life of hope, Christ does make a difference. St. Paul, in his letter to the Romans, gives us a formula for allowing Christ to enter into the struggles and sufferings of life that are inevitable. He says that as children of God, we are "heirs as well: heirs of God, heirs with Christ, if only we suffer with him so as to be glorified with him" (Rom. 8:17). St. Paul considers "the sufferings of the present to be as nothing compared with the glory to be revealed in us" (Rom. 8:18).

"Creation was made subject to futility, not of its own accord but by him who subjected it; yet not without hope because the world itself will be freed from its slavery to corruption and share in the glorious freedom of the children of God" (Rom. 8:20-21).

Christ came to liberate us from all that confines us: sin, suffering, and death. He came to give us hope. His coming releases us from the fears, discouragement, disillusionment, anxiety, and oppression wrought by the sin of Adam and our own personal sins.

His coming does not mean that we no longer have to confront evil. It means we will learn better how to handle it. Jesus did not avoid evil. He faced it as an infant in the womb, hunted down because of who He was. He faced it all the way to the Cross.

St. Paul suggests that we will need to do the same, to "suffer with him so as to be glorified with him," knowing that the sufferings of the present are nothing compared with the glory to be revealed in us.

It is important, however, that when the inevitable sufferings hit us, we do not handle the suffering alone. We unite them with the sufferings of Christ. Then we allow Him to embrace us in our struggles. We are better able to handle the hard times, whatever they may be—economic and financial failures, personal relations struggles, family illnesses or deaths, lack of support from those we love, little or big misunderstandings, or miscommunications.

Christ is there to help us through every trial. He is our hope and our salvation.

For Reflection, Action, or Commitment

How does uniting our sufferings with the sufferings of Christ enable us to handle hard times?

Light a Candle

Let us pray: "Lord, watch over Your people, who come to You in confidence. Strengthen the hearts of those who hope in You. Give courage to those who falter because of their failures. Lead them along in this holy season of Advent closer to You in hope by the power of Your Holy Spirit. May they one day proclaim Your saving acts of kindness in Your eternal Kingdom. Amen."

Day 19

Fear of Death and Helping Others

Fr. Benedict Groeschel, priest, author, and counselor, put on his psychologist's hat when he made the observation that most of the neurotic fears, and even addictive behavior, of people are associated with death and the difficulty of coming to grips with it.[27]

It is our relationship with Christ and our relationship with people around us in need that helps us deal with the fear of death.

Jesus tells us to get ready for death in Matthew 25:31–46, in that final judgment scene when the Son of Man comes in all His glory and separates the sheep from the goats. Those who recognized and served Him in serving the stranger, the hungry, the thirsty, the sick, the imprisoned, and the naked are placed on His right side and inherit the Kingdom. Those who failed to do so are placed on His left and inherit eternal punishment.

If we want to get ready for death and be relieved of the fear of death, if we want to obtain hope in everlasting life, we can experience that hope by helping other people. Fr. Groeschel and I wrote about this topic in a little book of meditations called *When Did We See You, Lord?* published by Our Sunday Visitor press.

---

[27] EWTN meditation, aired September 18, 2010.

Fr. Groeschel wrote in his introduction that "the grace of love for the needy is one of the most precious and spiritually enriching gifts one can receive from God."[28] The season we are in now is one of the special times of the year when people think about the needs of other people. Certainly, such an attitude should pervade our thinking all through the year, not just at Advent and Christmas. Fr. Groeschel suggests that "those who bear the name 'Christian' but do not invest themselves in charity, in whatever way they can, are—according to so gentle a soul as Mother Teresa—in grave spiritual danger."

Those who help others in need bring physical, psychological, and spiritual help and hope to those in need, but also to themselves as well, as benefactors. Helping others is one of the greatest sources of hope in our lives and helps us radiate the hope of Christ to those who are in need.

For Reflection, Action, or Commitment
How does investing ourselves in charity help
us to overcome our fear of death?

Light a Candle

Let us pray: "Lord, watch over Your people, who come to You in confidence. Strengthen the hearts of those who hope in You. Give courage to those who falter because of their failures. Lead them along in this holy season of Advent closer to You in hope by the power of Your Holy Spirit. May they one day proclaim Your saving acts of kindness in Your eternal Kingdom. Amen."

[28] Robert J. Baker and Benedict J. Groeschel, *When Did We See You, Lord?* (Our Sunday Visitor, 2005).

Day 20

Passing Up an Opportunity to Serve

I like the story about Mother Teresa, now St. Teresa of Calcutta, being on her way to attend a conference on hunger in Bombay, India. On her way there, she got lost and arrived late. On her way into the conference, right in front of the conference site, where hundreds of people were talking about food distribution and hunger, Mother Teresa discovered a dying man.

With the help of one of her sisters, she picked the man up and took him home, comforting him and preparing him for death.

She never got to the conference on hunger, where people were talking about how in fifteen years they could have so much food, so much this, and so much that. She never made it into the midst of the lofty discussion, because Jesus stopped her at the entrance to the conference hall in the form of a dying man.

No doubt, participants of the conference had passed the same man by on their way into the building, but none of them had stopped, like those in the biblical account of the good Samaritan. They had places to go, things to do. But then, so did Mother Teresa.[29]

[29] Ibid., 42–43.

How easy it is for us to pass the buck when it comes to compassion and mercy! We have many reasons for letting someone else take on humanity's needs. We have many arguments as to why we shouldn't get involved. But are they good reasons?

There is one motivation for us to do as Mother Teresa did. That is to discover Jesus Christ lying on the sidewalk or the roadways of life, as He beckons for us to come to His rescue. He doesn't tell us to take Him down the street to the nearest Salvation Army, good though that may be. Rather, He tells us to take Him to our own homes or the nearest place to get some food or shelter. We will be judged for how we handle the sick, the hungry, the homeless, the naked, and the imprisoned. In this holy Advent season, can we bring a little more hope into our world by helping others? Can we bring a little more hope into our own lives by thinking less of ourselves and more of others? It's not an easy task. The Christ who comes to us in this Advent season will help us see Himself in the face of those in need and bring all of us hope.

For Reflection, Action, or Commitment

*Why am I tempted to pass the buck, to avoid
service with silence and inaction?*

Light a Candle

Let us pray: "Lord, watch over Your people, who come to You in confidence. Strengthen the hearts of those who hope in You. Give courage to those who falter because of their failures. Lead them along in this holy season of Advent closer to You in hope by the power of Your Holy Spirit. May they one day proclaim Your saving acts of kindness in Your eternal Kingdom. Amen."

Day 21

Hope for Addictive Behavior

Some years ago, when I was a pastor, parishioners of mine in St. Augustine, Florida, and the St. Vincent de Paul Society helped start a farm to get the street people passing through our town off the street. We called the farm the "St. Vincent de Paul farm" and the community residing there "Our Lady of Hope community." There are now two farm community houses for women and one for men in that area, and there is another men's community near Hanceville, Alabama.

The reason for the success of the project comes down to a religious sister by the name of Mother Elvira Petrozzi. I met her in Italy after I discovered that we didn't have a handle on addictive behavior, and I heard about her Cenacolo community and its farms.

Mother Elvira doesn't approach addictive behavior quite the way most other people do. She centers her approach around the hopeful message of Jesus Christ and the resources of our Catholic Faith: the Sacrament of Reconciliation; Holy Mass; devotion to the Blessed Mother; hard, physical, manual labor; heavy discipline; and the support of a community of brothers and sisters in Christ. She doesn't charge those who make the three-year commitment, but she does ask for a lot of involvement from the person entering her community and that person's family members. It is a little like a monastic way of life and a basic training program for the Marines.

I've seen people go from despair to hope, from darkness to light, and from addictive behavior to charitable behavior. But it takes time and a lot of hope, which comes from a very heavy life of prayer.

Mother Elvira's philosophy is that if a person has to eat three times a day to nourish the body, a person also needs to eat (pray) at least three times to nourish the soul. All community members (in each of over seventy communities throughout the world) pray daily before the Blessed Sacrament. Devotion to the Blessed Mother is a major component of the life of prayer. There is hope for healing for people struggling with addictions and other problems. Why not add prayer to the rehabilitative regimen, as Mother Elvira Petrozzi does?[30]

For Reflection, Action, or Commitment

What insights of Mother Elvira do you find helpful?

Light a Candle

Let us pray: "Lord, watch over Your people, who come to You in confidence. Strengthen the hearts of those who hope in You. Give courage to those who falter because of their failures. Lead them along in this holy season of Advent closer to You in hope by the power of Your Holy Spirit. May they one day proclaim Your saving acts of kindness in Your eternal Kingdom. Amen."

[30] Please pray for Mother Elvira Petrozzi, who was called to eternal life on August 3, 2023.

Week 4

Day 22

The Saints: Models of Hope

The saints are special models for the life of Christ. In their lifetime, they were people of great hope. Against great odds and in the face of many obstacles, they carried on and never gave up, knowing Christ was with them every step of the way.

The saints are there for us today, encouraging us, supporting us, and walking with us in faith, hope, and love.

"In the life of each one of us," Pope Benedict XVI said, "there are very dear persons, to whom we feel particularly close; some are already in Gods arms; others still share with us the journey of life: they are our parents, relatives, educators. They are persons to whom we have done good or from whom we have received good. They are persons we know we can count on."

The pope says that "it is ... important to have travel companions on the journey of our Christian life.... A spiritual director, a confessor, persons with whom we can share the experience of faith." He is also thinking of "the Virgin Mary and of the saints. Each one," says the pope, "should have a saint that is familiar to him, to whom he feels close with prayer and intercession, but also to imitate him or her."

The pope invites us to know the saints better, "beginning with the one whose name" we bear, "by reading his life" and his writings.

We can be certain that they will become good guides to love the Lord ever more and valid aids for our "human and Christian growth." The pope has a special devotion to the saints whose names he bears, Joseph (from his baptismal name) and Benedict (the name he chose as pope). He also has a great devotion to St. Augustine.

What is your saint's name? Do you have a special devotion to various saints? When I was in the Diocese of Charleston, South Carolina, our diocesan patron was St. John the Baptist. Here in Birmingham, our diocesan patrons are St. Paul and St. John Vianney. My personal patron is St. Robert Bellarmine. Let us look to the saints of the past and present as models for life, as models of hope. They want to help us hope always in the Lord and serve us as great examples of the virtue of hope.

For Reflection, Action, or Commitment

What saint helps me to hope? What
about my own patron saint?

Light a Candle

Let us pray: "Lord, watch over Your people, who come to You in confidence. Strengthen the hearts of those who hope in You. Give courage to those who falter because of their failures. Lead them along in this holy season of Advent closer to You in hope by the power of Your Holy Spirit. May they one day proclaim Your saving acts of kindness in Your eternal Kingdom. Amen."

Day 23

Having Recourse to Angels and Archangels

The famous bishop of Geneva St. Francis de Sales had a particular devotion to his guardian angel. He celebrated the feast of the Guardian Angels with special care and piety. He looked to his guardian angel for blessing in the most important actions in his life. He had devotion not only to his own guardian angel but also to the angels of his friends. He even had devotion to the angels of those who had left the Church; and in his disputes with the Huguenots, he invoked their angels.

When he was absent from his diocese, he commended the diocese to the care of his holy angel, and he never failed to recognize the angels protecting the kingdoms, provinces, or parishes he entered.

In the confessional, he frequently invoked the guardian angel of his penitent. In his letters to friends, he recommended devotion to their guardian angel. In this world, he said, the angels attend to almost everything, as they are the messengers of God, and invisible. How much happens for good in our lives because of our guardian angels! How much they assist us in maintaining a disposition of hope and joy in serving the Lord!

I was installed as bishop of the Diocese of Birmingham on October 2, 2007, the feast of the Guardian Angels. Previously, I had been ordained a bishop for the Diocese of Charleston, South Carolina, on September 29, 1999, the feast of the archangels Michael, Raphael, and Gabriel. I pray daily to my guardian angel and to St. Michael.

I offer for your consideration the fact of the angels being special emissaries and ambassadors of hope. They do not let us be caught in a web of negativism, pessimism, or defeatism, but rather one of realism, optimism, and hope. They help us to identify problems where they are and to find our way to the proper solutions without fear or anxiety, but rather hope. May I recommend as a speedy deliverance from the bondage of a negative attitude and a negative spirit, frequent prayers to the angels, who are sent by God precisely to bring us greater hope and greater joy in all we do for the Kingdom of God.

For Reflection, Action, or Commitment
Do I pray to my guardian angel? Why or why not?

Light a Candle

Let us pray: "Lord, watch over Your people, who come to You in confidence. Strengthen the hearts of those who hope in You. Give courage to those who falter because of their failures. Lead them along in this holy season of Advent closer to You in hope by the power of Your Holy Spirit. May they one day proclaim Your saving acts of kindness in Your eternal Kingdom. Amen."

Day 24

The Holy Eucharist and Hope

The greatest source of hope on this side of eternity is the Sacrament of hope, the Sacrament of encounter with Christ that is the Holy Eucharist. The document of the Second Vatican Council that begins with the words *joy* and *hope*, *Gaudium et Spes*, says that "Christ left to his followers a pledge of ... hope and food for the journey in the sacrament of faith, in which natural elements, the fruits of human cultivation, are changed into his glorified Body and Blood, as a supper of brotherly and sisterly communion and a foretaste of the heavenly banquet."[31]

Those who frequent this Sacrament, receiving it often, if not daily, know that one of the fruits of the Sacrament is the virtue of hope. *Gaudium et Spes* refers to this Sacrament as a "pledge of hope and food for the journey" that Christ left to His followers.

This document of Vatican II opened with these words: "The joys and hopes, the grief and anguish of the people of our time, especially of those who are poor or afflicted, are the joys and hopes, the grief and anguish of the followers of Christ as well. Nothing

---

[31] Vatican Council II, Pastoral Constitution on the Church in the Modern World *Gaudium et Spes* (December 7, 1965), no. 38.

that is genuinely human fails to find an echo in their hearts. For theirs is a community of people united in Christ and guided by the Holy Spirit in their pilgrimage towards the Father's kingdom, bearers of a message of salvation for all of humanity."[32]

In the general intercessions at holy Mass, we bring the "joys and hopes, the grief and anguish of the people of our time, especially of those who are poor or afflicted." We name those needs and address them to God our Father, through the Son, and in the power of the Holy Spirit. We know that those pleas to God register with Him, as they come directly to God the Father through the Sacred Heart of Jesus, the compassionate and merciful heart of Christ.

When we bring our prayers and petitions to Holy Mass, we should trust that they are heard by God and that God will bring a most fitting response in His good time and in His unique way in His providential plan to all the prayers of our hearts. We might take them to Christ with the added prayer: "Jesus, I trust in You."

For Reflection, Action, or Commitment

Do I bring my special needs to Holy Mass and entrust them to the care of the Lord?

Light a Candle

Let us pray: "Lord, watch over Your people, who come to You in confidence. Strengthen the hearts of those who hope in You. Give courage to those who falter because of their failures. Lead them along in this holy season of Advent closer to You in hope by the power of Your Holy Spirit. May they one day proclaim Your saving acts of kindness in Your eternal Kingdom. Amen."

[32] Ibid., no. 1.

Day 25

St. John the Baptist, Emissary of Hope

In our final days of Advent, we reflect on the holy people who paved the way with their hopefulness for the coming of Christ. First among them is St. John the Baptist, the precursor of the Lord, the one who paved the way for His coming through his penitential lifestyle and his preaching of the truth, no matter what.

John and his followers fasted and prayed, living on little—in John's case, on grasshoppers and wild honey. He lived this way in anticipation and hope for the coming of the Messiah. As we anticipate great events, like the feast of Christ's birth, there is a penitential spirit in our preparations. The color purple reflects our penitential period of preparation. What goes with this sacred time may not be eating grasshoppers and wild honey, but there should be some effort at suggesting that we are in a holding pattern of hope and expectation. We are not in a celebratory mood yet. St. John sets the tone for us here.

He also sets the tone in helping us lead lives of integrity, as he did. We can truly hope that the Messiah is coming into our lives if we have discarded the cobwebs of selfishness and sinfulness, replacing them with honesty, integrity, truthfulness, and charity. What is lived on the outside must reflect what is true on the inside.

We are called to speak the truth. We are called to live the truth. And we probably have a ways to go in our journey toward integrity of life. So we appeal to St. John the Baptist to help us on this front.

Probably a little more prayer and a little more fasting will help us, as it helped this special saint of the Advent season.

I got to know St. John the Baptist well when I was bishop of Charleston, South Carolina. He was the patron of the cathedral there and patron of the diocese, and his picture hung in the chapel of my private residence. He reminded me of my call as a bishop to live a life of penance and integrity. In so doing, he helped me maintain a perspective of hope. We all know the Lord is just around the corner for those who hope in Him, as did St. John the Baptist.

For Reflection, Action, or Commitment

Do I need to do a little more praying or fasting in this holy season of Advent to prepare in hopefulness for the coming of Christ?

Light a Candle

Let us pray: "Lord, watch over Your people, who come to You in confidence. Strengthen the hearts of those who hope in You. Give courage to those who falter because of their failures. Lead them along in this holy season of Advent closer to You in hope by the power of Your Holy Spirit. May they one day proclaim Your saving acts of kindness in Your eternal Kingdom. Amen."

Day 26

The People of Hope Who Greeted Jesus

In this Advent season, we meditate on the figures of Simeon and Anna, who had the blessing of waiting in expectation and hope for the coming of the Messiah and were there to greet Jesus when His parents presented Him in the temple. Simeon is described as righteous and pious, awaiting the "consolation of Israel" (Luke 2:25). The Holy Spirit had revealed to him "that he would not experience death until he had seen the anointed of the lord" (v. 26). In joy, he prays, "Now, master you can dismiss your servant in peace; you have fulfilled your word. For my eyes have witnessed your saving deed displayed for all the peoples to see: a revealing light to the gentiles, the glory of your people Israel" (vv. 29–32).

The eighty-four-year-old widow Anna, daughter of Phanuel of the tribe of Asher, came to the temple constantly, worshipping day and night in fasting and prayer (see Luke 2:37). She was a woman of hope, and her prayer of hope was rewarded with a vision of the Messiah. "She gave thanks to God and talked about the child to all who looked forward to the deliverance of Jerusalem" (v. 38).

Then there were the magi. Pope Benedict refers to them in *Spe Salvi*. He tells us that St. Gregory Nazianzen says of them that "at the very moment when the magi, guided by the star, adored Christ the new king, astrology came to an end, because the stars were now moving in the orbit determined by Christ.... This scene, in fact overturns the world-view of that time, which in a different way has become fashionable once again today. It is not the elemental spirits of the universe, the laws of matter, which ultimately govern the world and mankind, but a personal God governs the stars, that is, the universe; it is not the laws of matter and of evolution that have the final say, but reason, will, love—a Person."[33] The magi found a new way to hope in the Christ child of Bethlehem.

And the shepherds, watching in their fields by night, though not looking for the Messiah, had simple enough hearts to receive a message of hope. That message can come to anyone at any time if one's heart is open and disposed, as were theirs.

For Reflection, Action, or Commitment

Would I have been one of those hopeful people who awaited the coming of the Messiah and welcomed Him?

Light a Candle

Let us pray: "Lord, watch over Your people, who come to You in confidence. Strengthen the hearts of those who hope in You. Give courage to those who falter because of their failures. Lead them along in this holy season of Advent closer to You in hope by the power of Your Holy Spirit. May they one day proclaim Your saving acts of kindness in Your eternal Kingdom. Amen."

---

[33] Benedict XVI, Encyclical *Spe Salvi* (November 30, 2007), no. 5.

Day 27

Mary and Joseph: Advent Models of Hope

Among the great figures of Advent is Joseph, from the town of Nazareth in Galilee, of the house and lineage of David (see Luke 2:4), espoused to Mary. He is an upright man, a man of hope, who had to place a lot of trust in God to fulfill the role ahead of him, which was described in a dream by an angel who told him that the child to be born of Mary was conceived by the power of the Holy Spirit. He is to name the child Jesus, "because he will save his people from their sins" (Matt. 1:21–22). Joseph is presented as a man who trusted in God at every moment, difficult though his role was.

St. Joseph is the patron of the universal Church, guiding the Church through the vicissitudes of history, as he guided and protected his foster son, Jesus. Friends of mine in the Cenacolo community, serving people struggling with addictions, pray to him every evening before supper. They bow down to the floor in their chapel and say these words: *"San Giuseppe, grazie; provede per noi."* ("St. Joseph, thank you; provide for us.") St. Joseph always comes through for them. He will always come through for us too, because he was a man of hope and trust in God. He wants us to be the same.

Mary holds many titles of honor, but a special title is Our Lady of Hope or Mother of Hope.

Pope Benedict highlights the role of Mary as a figure of hope. He says that "the true stars of our life are the people who have lived good lives. They are lights of hope. Certainly," he says, "Jesus Christ is the true light.... But to reach him we also needs lights close by—people who shine with his light and so guide us along our way. Who more than Mary could be a star of hope for us? With her 'yes' she opened the door of our world to God himself; she became the living Ark of the Covenant, in whom God took flesh, became one of us, and pitched his tent among us (cf. Jn 1:14)."[34]

When presented with the invitation to be the Mother of the Messiah, the Mother of God, Mary, understandably wondered and questioned how such a role could be hers, but she never doubted—unlike Zechariah, the father of John the Baptist, when confronted with the invitation to fatherhood late in life. His questioning led to lack of trust. Mary "trusted that the Lord's words to her would be fulfilled" (Luke 1:45).

Let us look to Mary and Joseph as true models of hope for us in this holy Advent season.

For Reflection, Action, or Commitment

Why are Mary and Joseph great models of hope for us? How does prayer to them inspire hope in us?

---

[34] Ibid., no. 49.

Light a Candle

Let us pray: "Lord, watch over Your people, who come to You in confidence. Strengthen the hearts of those who hope in You. Give courage to those who falter because of their failures. Lead them along in this holy season of Advent closer to You in hope by the power of Your Holy Spirit. May they one day proclaim Your saving acts of kindness in Your eternal Kingdom. Amen."

PRAYER TO OUR LADY AND MOTHER OF JOYFUL HOPE

O you, Our lady of joyful hope, we entrust the priests, deacons, seminarians, religious men and women, laity, and all the people of the world, in their joys and their sorrows, their triumphs and their defeats, their successes and their failures. As Mother of Christ and Mother of the Church, you are also Mother to all who call upon you in their need. You are the Mother of all races and all people.

Help our universal human family and all our families to draw closer together; help our youth to find meaning, purpose, and direction in life; help our frail elderly to know you are with them; help our sick, poor, abandoned, addicted, and unborn to be rescued by your love for them reaching out through us.

Lead us all closer to your Son, Our Lord, our Savior, and our God, Who is present with us in the most holy Eucharist. Through our prayers to you, Mother of joyful hope, especially the prayer of the Rosary, help us to become people of hope and of joy, radiating God's love

for us always, in your Son, Jesus Christ. In His powerful name and with your special intercession, we pray.
Amen.[35]

[35] Imprimatur: Most Reverend Robert J. Baker, S.T.D. Bishop of
Birmingham, August 15, 2012; Birmingham Catholic Press, Inc.
Diocese of Birmingham in Alabama, P.O. Box 10822, Birmingham,
Alabama 35202.

Day 28

Christ Our Hope: Emmanuel

The great author of hope, the psalmist, boldly proclaims that "God is our refuge and our strength, an ever-present help in distress. Thus, we do not fear, though earth be shaken and mountains quake to the depths of the sea, Though its waters rage and foam and mountains totter at its surging" (Ps. 46:2–4).

"The Lord of hosts is with us" (v. 4), says the psalmist, and how right he is! Those words take flesh with the coming of God into this world in Jesus. God crept up on humanity and went beyond the wildest imaginings of the psalmist, or the Prophet Isaiah, who told of a sign, promised by the Lord: "The virgin shall be with child, and bear a son, and shall name him Emmanuel" (Isa. 7:14). Matthew's Gospel has the angel recall this prophecy to Joseph in a dream, saying that "all this happened to fulfill what the lord had said through the Prophet: 'The Virgin shall be with child and give birth to a son, and they shall call him Emmanuel,' a name which means, 'God is with us'" (Matt. 1:22–23).

The single most important reason for our hope, which underlines all others, is the advent, the coming, of Christ into this world as "Emmanuel," as "God with us." Christ arrives on the scene to help us through every trial and tribulation, every source of suffering and distress. He, Christ, is our hope and our salvation.

His identity with us was to baffle the people of His time and all time. "The Word became flesh and made his dwelling among us, and we have seen his glory: the glory of an only son coming from the Father, filled with enduring love" (John 1:14). "God so loved the world that he gave his only son that whoever believes in him may not die but may have eternal life" (John 3:16). That message is powerful, and it will take more than a day, it will take a lifetime, to digest. Emmanuel, "God with us," God becoming one with us, divinity united with humanity in Jesus. This is the advent that we celebrate in a powerful way on Christmas Day!

And we, in turn, are called to translate that reality of God's love by activating it in our own lives through the love of God and our neighbor.

During his visit to England, Pope Benedict spoke to some four thousand young Catholic students in London, and he told them that "we need to have the courage to place our deepest hopes in God alone, not in money, in a career, in worldly success, or our relationships with others, but in God. Only He can satisfy the deepest needs of our hearts."[36]

Today, we entrust the deepest needs of our hearts to the Emmanuel of the first Christmas Day, and in turn, we bring His light, His love, and His very presence as Emmanuel, "God with us," into the world in which we live.

Christ is our hope, and through His love for us, we bring Christ, our hope, into a world that is trying to find meaning and

---

[36] Benedict XVI, "Address of the Holy Father to Pupils" (September 17, 2010).

hope. Let us celebrate today, and long into the future, this Christ Who is "God with us," born in Bethlehem. He is our hope and our salvation!

For Reflection, Action, or Commitment

Reflect on these words from St. Paul's Letter to the Romans:

Do not grow slack but be fervent in spirit; he whom you serve is the lord. Rejoice in hope, be patient under trial, persevere in prayer. (12:11–12)

Reflect on these words from a meditation by St. Patrick:

Christ with me, Christ before me, Christ behind me
Christ in me, Christ beneath me, Christ above me,
Christ on my right, Christ on my left,
Christ when I lie down, Christ when I sit down,
Christ when arise,
Christ in the heart of every man who thinks of me,
Christ in the mouth of everyone who speaks of me,
Christ in every eye that sees me,
Christ in every ear that hears me.

At this point light the white Christ candle of hope,
and blow out the four Advent candles,
signifying the end of the Advent season
and the beginning of the Christmas season.

"Remember your word to your servant
by which you give me hope.
This is my comfort in affliction,
your promise that gives me life"
(Ps. 119:49–50).

Hope came into the world
with the incarnation of
the Son of God.

— Pope Francis

MEDITATIONS FOR THE CHRISTMAS SEASON

Walking down Broad Street in Charleston, South Carolina, approximately one day after Christmas, I nearly avoided getting hit by a Christmas tree being thrown off a second-story balcony. For that person, Christmas was over Christmas Day. For Christians, Christmas is not over on Christmas Day. Christmas is a season! And it lasts from Christmas Day until the feast of the Baptism of the Lord, which is a movable feast.

You are invited to enter into the glorious celebration of the Christmas season with the help of our meditations and prayers. Following each meditation, light a Christ candle of hope and pray a prayer such as the one provided with these meditations.

December 25

Christmas Day

My friends, I remind you that Christmas is not just a day. It is a season.

The celebration of the greatest event of all time is upon us once again. This day is called by different names: the solemnity of the Incarnation, the feast of the Birth of Christ, and Christmas Day. Whatever the name, it's important to realize that the Church invites us to celebrate this great event not just on Christmas Day but also throughout the Christmas season. And that season extends to the feast of the Baptism of the Lord.

It would be tragic if people celebrated Christmas just one day because this is such an important feast.

I was walking down the street in the historic and beautiful city of Charleston, South Carolina, just one day after Christmas, and someone was throwing out their Christmas tree from a second-floor balcony. It nearly landed on me.

That gesture dramatically reminded me that Christmas is over for many people right after Christmas. For dedicated followers of Jesus Christ, it's not over so quickly.

In the creed of holy Mass on Christmas Day, we all genuflect when we profess these words: "by the power of the Holy Spirit He was born of the Virgin Mary and became man." "*Et incarnatus est de Spiritu Santo ex Maria Virgine, et Homo Factus Est.*"

Those are some pretty powerful words, and we need more than a day to reflect on them. We need a season: the entire Christmas season.

With the help of the figures of the Christmas crib, universally displayed in our churches and our homes this Christmas season, we are led to ponder the great mystery of God becoming man in Jesus.

"God loved the world so much that he gave his only Son so that everyone who believes in him may not die but have eternal life" (John 3:16).

With the help of your Christmas crib, meditate on those words this Christmas day, and this Christmas season.

Let us pray:

CHRIST CANDLE OF HOPE PRAYER

God, our loving Father, You sent Your Son, Jesus Christ, into this world to counter all the forces of evil—sin, suffering, and death—and to overcome evil with the force of good, hatred with the power of love, Your great love for us in Jesus.

Help us never to curse the darkness, but to join with You in bringing Your light into this world, the light that is Your Son, born of the Virgin Mary, in Bethlehem.

Help us to be instruments of Your light and love by doing one special act of kindness or by being Your special instrument of reconciliation this Christmas season.

May the Christ candle we light symbolize our desire to bring light into a world of darkness and hope into a world of despair.

We ask this through Christ Our Lord. Amen.

December 26

The Christmas Crib

Dear friends, I bet most of you have a crib set in your home this Christmas season. Certainly, there is one displayed in your parish church or monastery chapel. This is one of the most popular symbols of the Christmas season. And I think that is great! The term *crib* is generally a synonym for the whole nativity scene. The French term *crèche* is often used as well. The Roman Basilica of St. Mary Major has had five small boards of Levantine sycamore, possibly since the seventh century, that are venerated as being from the crib of Christ.

St. Francis of Assisi was the person who really launched devotion to the crib with his *presepio* at Greccio in Italy back in 1223. St. Francis used lived figures to bring home the message of God's love portrayed by the nativity setting. The Franciscans and others promoted the custom, and it spread widely on the continent after the fourteenth century. By the Baroque era, the devotion was pretty much in place throughout Christianity, and even secular figures got added to those of the Holy Family, the shepherds, and the magi. Missionaries from Europe brought the crib custom to the Americas. And you are the beneficiaries of this wonderful custom today.

Franciscans in Assisi display the crib scene all year around next to their Santa Maria deli Angeli Basilica, as does Mother Angelica at her monastery in Hanceville, Alabama.

Keep your Christmas crib displayed throughout the Christmas season. But don't just look at it. Meditate on its meaning. That crib set and all the figures in it have a message for you this Christmas season.

Let's say a prayer that helps us translate the message of love in this Christmas crib into the world in which we live, and light a Christ candle of hope that reminds us of the Christ child of Bethlehem.

Christ Candle of Hope Prayer

God, our loving Father, You sent Your Son, Jesus Christ, into this world to counter all the forces of evil—sin, suffering, and death—and to overcome evil with the force of good, hatred with the power of love, Your great love for us in Jesus.

Help us never to curse the darkness, but to join with You in bringing Your light into this world, the light that is Your Son, born of the Virgin Mary, in Bethlehem.

Help us to be instruments of Your light and love by doing one special act of kindness or by being Your special instrument of reconciliation this Christmas season.

May the Christ candle we light symbolize our desire to bring light into a world of darkness and hope into a world of despair.

We ask this through Christ Our Lord. Amen.

December 27

Emmanuel, "God Is with Us"

In an ordination homily for five new bishops at St. Peter's Basilica in Rome on September 12, 2009, Pope Benedict told the future bishops that "the first and essential good which man needs is closeness to God himself." And he said that the kingdom of God is "not something 'next to' God, not some worldly condition; it is simply the presence of God himself, which is the truly healing force."

One of the special titles of the Christ of the Christmas season is "Emmanuel," which means "God with us."

The proclamation that God is with us in Jesus came in a special way in our Christmas liturgies, but that proclamation comes to us all through the Christmas season, and at every holy Mass.

God is here in the holy Eucharist to give healing and hope to every situation of life.

For many people, God may seem far away or remote this Christmas season. An illness, a death in the family, a loss of a job, a problematic marriage, a son or daughter or spouse addicted to drugs or alcohol, or the doctor's report of a serious life-threatening or terminal illness may lead a person to question where God is at this moment. God is here. God is near. He is Emmanuel, God with us in Jesus.

The Sacraments of the Church are infallible signs of His divine presence among us. Through those Sacraments, especially the Holy Eucharist, we have the divine assurance that God is with us, just as He was with Mary and Joseph, with the shepherds and the magi, that first Christmas.

Let us joyfully proclaim, with our liturgies and with our lives, this Christmas season, that Jesus Christ is truly Emmanuel, God with us!

And let us now pray the Christ Candle of Hope Prayer, which helps us proclaim that God is with us in Jesus.

CHRIST CANDLE OF HOPE PRAYER

God, our loving Father, You sent Your Son, Jesus Christ, into this world to counter all the forces of evil—sin, suffering, and death—and to overcome evil with the force of good, hatred with the power of love, Your great love for us in Jesus.

Help us never to curse the darkness, but to join with You in bringing Your light into this world, the light that is Your Son, born of the Virgin Mary, in Bethlehem.

Help us to be instruments of Your light and love by doing one special act of kindness or by being Your special instrument of reconciliation this Christmas season.

May the Christ candle we light symbolize our desire to bring light into a world of darkness and hope into a world of despair.

We ask this through Christ Our Lord. Amen.

December 28

Feast of the Holy Innocents

It's hard to imagine how a king could be threatened by a little infant, but that is what happened when King Herod feared for his throne. He thought he had a rival on his hands in the person of this little infant, Jesus.

Already at birth, there was a price tag on the head of Jesus. And Herod goes so far in his fury as to order the massacre of all who resembled Jesus in gender and age.

The Holy Innocents become the first martyrs for the cause of the Kingdom. They were the first to pay the price for the entrance of the King of kings and Lord of lords into this world.

Why are we so hard on infants? What harm do we fear from them?

Are they a threat to our life and lifestyle, as they were to King Herod?

Can we not find a place for them and welcome them into our society?

Jesus had a special regard for little children. He told His disciples that they

had to change and become like little children to enter the Kingdom of God.

Do we snuff out their existence precisely because they most resemble the Kingdom of God? Are they a threat because they are closer to God than we are?

A culture that denies birthright to innocent infants is a culture like the one that prevailed at the time of Herod. We are that culture.

We are grateful to Mary and Joseph for heeding the warning signs around them and fleeing to Egypt to protect the one placed into their care.

May all of us be like them and do all we can to protect the innocent unborn and born children, whose lives are threatened by an indifferent society.

Let us pray the Christ Candle of Hope Prayer for them.

Christ Candle of Hope Prayer

God, our loving Father, You sent Your Son, Jesus Christ, into this world to counter all the forces of evil—sin, suffering, and death—and to overcome evil with the force of good, hatred with the power of love, Your great love for us in Jesus.

Help us never to curse the darkness, but to join with You in bringing Your light into this world, the light that is Your Son, born of the Virgin Mary, in Bethlehem.

Help us to be instruments of Your light and love by doing one special act of kindness or by being Your special instrument of reconciliation this Christmas season.

May the Christ candle we light symbolize our desire to bring light into a world of darkness and hope into a world of despair.

We ask this through Christ Our Lord. Amen.

December 29

Continued Meditation on the Christmas Crib

My friends, today we continue our reflections on the Christmas crib, most likely displayed in your home, as it is in mine. Let's take a look at the most important figure displayed in our Christmas crib. It is the infant Jesus.

The Christ child has many titles. In the church of Ara Coeli in Rome, He is called the Santo Bambino. In Colombia, He is referred to as the Divino Nino. In India, He's the Infant Jesus. In Mexico, the Santo Nino de Atocha. In the Philippines, the Child of Cebu. In Czechoslovakia, He is the Infant of Prague.

Why does an infant get so much attention at Christmas time? Because from the dawn of Christianity to our own day and time, the Divine Child has helped us understand God's love for us so much easier.

The American saint Katharine Drexel once said that God has "become a little infant so that you may love him without fear."

Author George Weigel says that babies have the special capacity to drain the rest of us of egocentricity and cynicism. That is why God decided to enter the world as a newborn. "The God with a human face began the climactic portion of his salvific journey

through history as a baby," says Weigel, "calling others out of themselves as only babies can do."

Every year, the Christmas crèche "calls us to ponder the law of the gift written on the human heart by the God who is love."

Take the time to look at the infant in the crib, and ask Him to drain you of any egocentricity or cynicism that might lurk in your life or your world.

And then light the Christ candle of hope and say a prayer that the *Divino Nino* might help you bring light and hope into our world.

CHRIST CANDLE OF HOPE PRAYER

God, our loving Father, You sent Your Son, Jesus Christ, into this world to counter all the forces of evil—sin, suffering, and death—and to overcome evil with the force of good, hatred with the power of love, Your great love for us in Jesus.

Help us never to curse the darkness, but to join with You in bringing Your light into this world, the light that is Your Son, born of the Virgin Mary, in Bethlehem.

Help us to be instruments of Your light and love by doing one special act of kindness or by being Your special instrument of reconciliation this Christmas season.

May the Christ candle we light symbolize our desire to bring light into a world of darkness and hope into a world of despair.

We ask this through Christ Our Lord. Amen.

December 30

Feast of the Holy Family—Images in Your Christmas Crib

Welcome, friends, to our continued reflections on your Christmas crib, which graces your church and your home this Christmas season.

Central to the images in that crib setting is the Holy Family: Jesus, Mary, and Joseph.

They are the principal actors in the drama of our salvation, with the central figure being the Infant Jesus.

Pope St. John Paul II said that the future of humanity passes by way of the family. That is because the Holy Family presents us with hope for the family and hope for humanity.

Pope Benedict reminded us that "the family is the privileged setting where every person learns to give and receive love."

It takes a family for us to learn the lessons of love. It takes the Holy Family to model for us the meaning of giving and receiving love.

The infant Jesus showered love on His parents from the moment of His conception in the womb of His Mother, Mary. The first great love was Jesus' love for Mary, and then, of course, for His foster father, Joseph.

But then, too, Jesus was on the receiving end of love—the love of his parents, the respectful love that they had for the only begotten Son of God the Father.

How special they were to Him and He to them. For all eternity, this Holy Family will be special, unique, and the icon of the perfect family.

We need, society needs, this family to draw strength and support for family life. What does it mean to be a loving husband or wife, a gentle parent, or a caring son or daughter?

Take your questions like this to your Christmas crib on the feast of the Holy Family and during the Christmas season. Where does your family hurt? What relationship needs healing?

I bet the Holy Family has an answer to help bring reconciliation and peace to your family this Christmas season.

Let us pray:

Christ Candle of Hope Prayer

God, our loving Father, You sent Your Son, Jesus Christ, into this world to counter all the forces of evil—sin, suffering, and death—and to overcome evil with the force of good, hatred with the power of love, Your great love for us in Jesus.

Help us never to curse the darkness, but to join with You in bringing Your light into this world, the light that is Your Son, born of the Virgin Mary, in Bethlehem.

Help us to be instruments of Your light and love by doing one special act of kindness or by being Your special instrument of reconciliation this Christmas season.

May the Christ candle we light symbolize our desire to bring light into a world of darkness and hope into a world of despair.

We ask this through Christ Our Lord. Amen.

December 31

The Messiah

There are certain times in our lives when we as Catholics are anointed with Holy Chrism: when we receive the Sacrament of Baptism, the Sacrament of Confirmation, and, if we are priests or bishops, the Sacrament of Holy Orders.

Like the kings of Israel, we are anointed.

The word *Messiah* comes from the Hebrew adjective *mashiah* and describes a person who is anointed with oil.

The word *Christ*, from the Greek word *christos*, means "the anointed one." It is our version of the Hebrew word for *Messiah*.

Jesus, for Christians, is *the Christ*, the anointed one, the long-awaited Messiah, Who would redeem His people from their sins.

The people of Israel had come in the course of centuries to look for a Messiah who would bring about God's definitive intervention in history and usher in a unique event for all time and eternity. Many Jewish people at the time of Jesus awaited *hammasiach*, "the anointed one," "the messiah," or in Greek, *o xristos*, "the Christ," Who would restore the throne of David and right the wrongs against the people of Israel. Matthew's Gospel tells us what the prophet has written: "And you, Bethlehem, land of Judah, are by no means least among the princes of Judah, since from you shall come a ruler who is to shepherd my people Israel" (Matt. 2:6).

Christians identify Jesus as that long-awaited Messiah. We are in continuity with our Jewish brethren in the expectation of the Messiah, but not in the identification of Jesus as the Messiah. Nothing is lost in the teaching of the Jewish Scriptures, which our Christian faith inherits, but something new is here.

The Kingdom of God is in our midst with the birth of Jesus. The Anointed One, the Messiah, the Christ is with us. Our look at the past history of the people of Israel is seen in a new light, and we look to the future with even greater hope and joy. Jesus is the Messiah, our long-awaited Savior. He is Our Lord and our God; He is Jesus, the Christ.

We pray to Him now the Christ Candle of Hope Prayer.

CHRIST CANDLE OF HOPE PRAYER

God, our loving Father, You sent Your Son, Jesus Christ, into this world to counter all the forces of evil—sin, suffering, and death—and to overcome evil with the force of good, hatred with the power of love, Your great love for us in Jesus.

Help us never to curse the darkness, but to join with You in bringing Your light into this world, the light that is Your Son, born of the Virgin Mary, in Bethlehem.

Help us to be instruments of Your light and love by doing one special act of kindness or by being Your special instrument of reconciliation this Christmas season.

May the Christ candle we light symbolize our desire to bring light into a world of darkness and hope into a world of despair.

We ask this through Christ Our Lord. Amen.

January 1

Solemnity of Mary, Mother of God

How special Mary is to the redemptive plan of God for the human race. As the Mother of God, Mary plays a unique and special role in the drama of salvation.

We meditate today on the solemnity of Mary, Mother of God, on this great woman of faith's role in our redemption.

Mary's greatest title is that of Mother of God. The Church grappled with her relationship with her Son at the Council of Ephesus in the year 431. That great council of the Church proclaimed that "Mary truly became the mother of God by the human conception of the Son of God in her womb." *Theotokos* was the Greek word for this role of Mary, literally meaning "the bearer of God."

The Swiss mystical writer Adrienne von Speyr wrote of Mary that "nothing in her opposes the redemptive action of the Son; rather everything places itself at his disposal to further and enhance it."

Wouldn't it be great if that could be said of us and our lives? Nothing in us opposes the redemptive action of God. Rather, we place our whole lives 100 percent at the service of God and His redemptive plan for the human race.

Mary let God take over her life totally. Her fiat, "thy will be done," was not just empty or fleeting words. It was a yes to God that would embrace everything, giving birth to the Son of God in her womb, and then taking on the challenges of helping the Kingdom of her Son reach out to all the ends of the earth.

Mary is still actively promoting her Son's mission. On occasion, she appears on the scene to remind us of her Son's will for humanity, His wishes for each one of us.

Pray to Mary daily, and in a special way, pray the holy Rosary, a prayer that reminds us of Mary's role in the plan of the Redeemer, of her role as the Mother of God. Mary never stops sharing stories with us about her Son's great love for us, each one of us, how His life had touched her life, and how His life touches ours today. Let Mary be your Mother too.

Let us pray with her a prayer of hope and joy.

CHRIST CANDLE OF HOPE PRAYER

God, our loving Father, You sent Your Son, Jesus Christ, into this world to counter all the forces of evil—sin, suffering, and death—and to overcome evil with the force of good, hatred with the power of love, Your great love for us in Jesus.

Help us never to curse the darkness, but to join with You in bringing Your light into this world, the light that is Your Son, born of the Virgin Mary, in Bethlehem.

Help us to be instruments of Your light and love by doing one special act of kindness or by being Your special instrument of reconciliation this Christmas season.

May the Christ candle we light symbolize our desire to bring light into a world of darkness and hope into a world of despair.

We ask this through Christ Our Lord. Amen.

January 2

Mary, the Model of Joy

We continue to look to our Christmas cribs, still displayed in our homes, for lessons for life during the Christmas season.

And we look once again at the figure of Mary. We always find her next to the infant Jesus.

She has a look of wonder and awe on her face in some Christmas figurines. In my Christmas crib, which is from Italy (the figures

are carved by a man named Ferràndiz), Mary is seated, with her hands folded and a smile on her face.

What I like about the figures in this Italian nativity set is the smiles on peoples' faces, as is the case with Mary.

Being close to Jesus makes us happy, hopeful, and joyful. How much joy there must have been in that first Christmas setting! So what if Jesus was born in a stable because there was no room in the inn! Mary was happy, happy because Jesus was near her. Pope Benedict once said the "first and essential good which man needs is closeness to God himself."

Mary had that with Jesus in her womb, and here with Jesus in the manger. That was enough for her. She didn't need all the trappings of what other mothers have during childbirth: a clean room, a nice bed for the child, plenty of linens, and warm clothing.

The heat would come from the animals huddled close by. But the warmth would also come from the love of the Christ child Himself.

Mary becomes the model of the happy, joyful disciple, close by her child in prayer. If Christ is close, if God is close to us, the battle is won. The first and essential good that human beings need was met in that stable that Christmas day.

Mary didn't complain to Joseph and criticize him because he hadn't found a better setting. She was so happy that Jesus was now born into this world. Her joy could not be contained. She wants us to be joyful this Christmas season too, no matter what our circumstances—poverty, sickness, loneliness, whatever. God is near; God is here. Take your cue from Mary! Rejoice and be glad!

Let us pray:

CHRIST CANDLE OF HOPE PRAYER

God, our loving Father, You sent Your Son, Jesus Christ, into this world to counter all the forces of evil—sin, suffering, and death—and to overcome evil with the force of good, hatred with the power of love, Your great love for us in Jesus.

Help us never to curse the darkness, but to join with You in bringing Your light into this world, the light that is Your Son, born of the Virgin Mary, in Bethlehem.

Help us to be instruments of Your light and love by doing one special act of kindness or by being Your special instrument of reconciliation this Christmas season.

May the Christ candle we light symbolize our desire to bring light into a world of darkness and hope into a world of despair.

We ask this through Christ Our Lord. Amen.

The Prince of Peace

One of the great titles for the Lord that we invoke and reflect on in this Christmas season is that of Prince of Peace.

The little infant of the Christmas crib appears so much at peace there, embraced by the love of God the Father and the Holy Spirit, surrounded by Jesus and Mary and the shepherds who came to adore Him. What a contrast between the Bethlehem of His era and the Bethlehem of ours, now a city of strife and tension, a veritable war zone.

With conflicts over territory, cultural heritage, and religious beliefs, hostility is constantly at a fever pitch, even in the church over the site of Jesus' birth, which was the center of a stand-off between the warring parties not long ago.

Who will bring peace to the Middle East and to Ukraine, to all the war-torn places of our world?

Hopefully, the Prince of Peace will by working through us. The consequences of our failure to succeed, with the Prince of Peace working in and through us, are catastrophic.

REJOICING IN OUR HOPE

We ask the Prince of Peace to join our prayer today with all people of goodwill, who pray for peace in our world and work for that peace.

Since peace starts in ourselves, in our homes, and in our families and communities, we ask the Prince of Peace to unite our hearts with His so that we may experience the peace of God within us. Only then can we share the peace of God with others.

Only then will we be instruments of peace in our world. Only then will we turn hatred in the world to love, injury to pardon, sadness to joy, darkness to light, and outer conflict to inner peace.

Let us light the Christ candle of hope for peace in our hearts and homes, peace in the Holy Land, and peace in our world; and then let us pray a prayer for hope and peace.

CHRIST CANDLE OF HOPE PRAYER

God, our loving Father, You sent Your Son, Jesus Christ, into this world to counter all the forces of evil—sin, suffering, and death—and to overcome evil with the force of good, hatred with the power of love, Your great love for us in Jesus.

Help us never to curse the darkness, but to join with You in bringing Your light into this world, the light that is Your Son, born of the Virgin Mary, in Bethlehem.

Help us to be instruments of Your light and love by doing one special act of kindness or by being Your special instrument of reconciliation this Christmas season.

May the Christ candle we light symbolize our desire to bring light into a world of darkness and hope into a world of despair.

We ask this through Christ Our Lord. Amen.

January 4

The Arms Race

The decision by the Russian government in February of 2023 to withdraw from a nuclear arms negotiation with the United States because of the United States' growing support of Ukraine in its resistance to Moscow was an alarming move that precipitated greater fears of a nuclear showdown on the horizon.

C-SPAN's *Washington Journal*, on February 22, 2023, invited a nuclear arms control expert, Daryl Kimball, to comment on the development.

Kimball noted that nuclear arms reduction talks between the United States and Russia have resulted in a greater reduction of nuclear weapons by both countries since the Cold War in the 1960s. However, both sides have more than enough weapons yet to destroy each other. Kimball added that the United States has enough nuclear weapons now to defend itself if attacked.

Additional problems are that China, like Russia, is refusing to enter into nuclear arms discussions.

Obviously, North Korea poses a threat by randomly flexing its muscle, with its constant release of missiles capable of carrying nuclear warheads.

Our recent popes have called on all governments to eliminate the use of nuclear weapons. Sounding this alarm makes eminently good sense. Arriving at this goal seems next to impossible without a lot of prayer and honest, continued, persistent negotiations. Hopefully, the Holy See will continue to offer its wisdom and skills to bring nations back to the bargaining table. The alternative is too disastrous to imagine.

On an apostolic journey of Pope Francis to war-torn Sudan (February 2023), Pope Francis said, "It is precisely for peace that we are called 'to work.' Jesus wants us to be peacemakers (cf. Mt. 5:9). He wants his church to be not only a sign and instrument of intimate union with God but also of the unity of the entire human family (cf. *Lumen Gentium* 1)."[37]

Pope Francis highlighted the importance of prayer as central to efforts for peace: "The great commitment of Christian communities to human development, solidarity, and peace would be fruitless without prayer. Indeed, we cannot promote peace without first invoking Jesus, the 'Prince of Peace' (Is 9:5)."[38]

During in-flight comments to journalists on his return trip from Sudan, Pope Francis noted that "the whole world is at war, and in the process of self-destruction.... We must stop in time, because one bomb leads to another, bigger one, then an even bigger, and in the escalation, you don't know where you will end up."[39]

We must take seriously the cautionary words of our Holy Father, pray hard, and do all we can to work for peace in our world!

Let us now pray the Christ Candle of Hope Prayer.

[37] Francis, "Apostolic Journey of His Holiness Pope Francis to the Democratic Republic of the Congo and South Sudan" (February 4, 2023).

[38] Ibid.

[39] Francis, "In-Flight Press Conference" (February 5, 2023).

CHRIST CANDLE OF HOPE PRAYER

God, our loving Father, You sent Your Son, Jesus Christ, into this world to counter all the forces of evil—sin, suffering, and death—and to overcome evil with the force of good, hatred with the power of love, Your great love for us in Jesus.

Help us never to curse the darkness, but to join with You in bringing Your light into this world, the light that is Your Son, born of the Virgin Mary, in Bethlehem.

Help us to be instruments of Your light and love by doing one special act of kindness or by being Your special instrument of reconciliation this Christmas season.

May the Christ candle we light symbolize our desire to bring light into a world of darkness and hope into a world of despair.

We ask this through Christ Our Lord. Amen.

January 5

Patience Breeds Hope

The saddest day for the pro-life movement each year was January 22, the day in 1973 that the US Supreme Court, in the landmark *Roe v. Wade* decision, ruled that the Constitution of the United States conferred the right to choose an abortion, thereby inaugurating the endorsement of the killing of unborn infants by the federal government. The argument was that the due process clause of the Fourteenth Amendment to the US Constitution provides a fundamental "right to privacy" that protects a pregnant woman's liberty to abort the fetus in her womb.

The following year, 1974, an attorney by the name of Nellie Gray helped organize what was to become a National March for Life in Washington, DC, each year, close to January 22. It was to become the largest and longest-running pro-life demonstration in the world. The *New York Times* gave Nellie Gray credit for popularizing the term *pro-life*.

This march began as a march composed of mostly young people. The Archdiocese of St. Louis, under the aegis of the diocesan director of pro-life activities, the future Archbishop Joseph Nauman, helped release hundreds of students from Catholic high schools to go to Washington for the March for Life. Other dioceses followed suit. Marches for life proliferated around the United States and the world.

Nellie Gray became ill on the stage of her last march for life and passed out. I was present on the stage when that happened. She died on August 13, 2012, but the march went on and on and on. God bless that great lady and the hundreds of thousands of people she inspired!

The pro-life movement only continued to grow because the arguments for the protection of the unborn were on the side of logic and truth, both morally and constitutionally.

Though there was precedence for overturning previous court decisions, legal jurisprudence generally supports the practice of *stare decisis*—that is, standing by what already has been decided by a high court. So it took great legal expertise, wisdom, and courage for five Supreme Court justices in the *Dobbs v. Jackson Women's Health Organization* case (2022) to uphold a ruling that the Constitution of the United States does not confer a right to abortion, thus overturning *Roe v. Wade* (1973) and *Planned Parenthood v. Casey* (1992).

The five justices who voted in the majority opinion of the Dobbs decision were subjected to harassment, protests, and life-threatening situations. They are modern-day heroes, along with the hundreds of thousands of people, young and old, who patiently marched in cold weather, sometimes under treacherous conditions, because they believed in the value of human life.

All of them proved that patience breeds hope, and hope brings change for the good!

Let us light a Christ candle of hope and pray for all those patient and courageous people!

CHRIST CANDLE OF HOPE PRAYER

God, our loving Father, You sent Your Son, Jesus Christ, into this world to counter all the forces of evil—sin, suffering, and death—and to overcome evil with the force of good, hatred with the power of love, Your great love for us in Jesus.

Help us never to curse the darkness, but to join with You in bringing Your light into this world, the light that is Your Son, born of the Virgin Mary, in Bethlehem.

Help us to be instruments of Your light and love by doing one special act of kindness or by being Your special instrument of reconciliation this Christmas season.

May the Christ candle we light symbolize our desire to bring light into a world of darkness and hope into a world of despair.

We ask this through Christ Our Lord. Amen.

January 6

Solemnity of the Epiphany

The word *epiphany* comes from the Greek word *epiphaneia*, which means "appearance" or "manifestation."

Today, we celebrate the manifestation of Jesus as the Christ, the Messiah, the Anointed One, to the Gentiles, represented by the magi.

In our Christmas cribs today are displayed three figures depicting the men from the East, described in chapter 2 of Matthew's Gospel as searching for the "newborn king of the Jews" (v. 2). When they found the child, they presented Him gifts of gold, frankincense, and myrrh. Such gifts would have been customary in the Orient as signs of homage.

We have before us the manifestation, the revelation, of Christ, the Son of God, to people of Gentile heritage.

You know, there are good epiphanies and bad ones. Good manifestations and bad ones.

This manifestation was of the presence of God.

There are other manifestations you and I experience daily that are manifestations of evil, which can come in the form of the temptations from the world, the flesh, and yes, the devil, who is the personification of evil.

The devil tries to keep himself hidden from us. He works best behind the scenes. On occasion, he manifests himself. The prayers and fasting and exorcisms of the Church make him manifest his presence. So we can know what form of evil is in our midst.

The greatest force to combat the evil we confront is the manifestation of the presence of Christ in our midst.

He came precisely to overcome all the forces of evil—sin, suffering, and death—in all their manifestations: the world, the flesh, and the devil.

Christ reveals Himself; and He manifests Himself to us today, as He did to the magi, in the Sacraments of His Church, especially the Holy Eucharist.

And these epiphanies are signs of hope for us and proofs to us that God is with us in Jesus, and He is more powerful than all the epiphanies of evil.

Let us light the Christ candle of hope in honor of Christ, Who was manifested to the world in Bethlehem and Who brings light and hope to all people of all generations in every part of the world.

Christ Candle of Hope Prayer

God, our loving Father, You sent Your Son, Jesus Christ, into this world to counter all the forces of evil—sin, suffering, and death—and to overcome evil with the force of good, hatred with the power of love, Your great love for us in Jesus.

Help us never to curse the darkness, but to join with You in bringing Your light into this world, the light that is Your Son, born of the Virgin Mary, in Bethlehem.

Help us to be instruments of Your light and love by doing one special act of kindness or by being Your special instrument of reconciliation this Christmas season.

May the Christ candle we light symbolize our desire to bring light into a world of darkness and hope into a world of despair.

We ask this through Christ Our Lord. Amen.

January 7

Working and Praying for Racial Harmony

In the wake of riots that erupted over racial issues in Ferguson, Missouri; Baltimore, Maryland; Los Angeles; Oakland; and Brooklyn, a symposium was held on March 3 and 4, 2016, at Beeson Divinity School on the campus of Samford University in Birmingham, Alabama, entitled "Black and White in America: How Deep the Divide?" This symposium was a modest effort to engage leaders from civil and religious communities in a discussion on the depth of the divide between blacks and whites in America and who among us is doing anything positive and creative about building bridges.

Birmingham is ground zero, historically, for the civil rights movement, and it seemed to be the ideal location to engage in that conversation.

It should be noted that more riots emerged throughout the United States after that important convocation.

This conference underlined the great divide that still exists, years after the passing of Dr. Martin Luther King Jr. and years after initial strides of progress had been made in racial harmony. The conference discussions took place in a spirit of openness, honesty, and civility, and it gave evidence that more conferences like this are needed throughout our country. The list of speakers and a published booklet of the conference talks and discussions are available from the Office of Black Catholics of the Diocese of Birmingham.

I acknowledge the contributions of Dr. Timothy George, then dean of the Beeson Divinity School, and Mayor William A. Bell Sr., then mayor of Birmingham, who assisted us in organizing that conference.

What became clear to me from that conference was that there were too few efforts for members of the black and white communities to actually seriously listen to each other. As a consequence, before my retirement as bishop of Birmingham in Alabama, I initiated listening sessions in both predominately black and predominately white parishes. People came to honestly air their concerns. There were many concerns on both sides. Strong feelings were still present.

The list of grievances went on, but only by listening did we begin to understand the attitudes behind the grievances. Then we could begin to understand why a racial divide still exists. The problems were on both sides, and they will only increase unless more listening and learning and praying is undertaken by all parties.

This is not to suggest that many people are not making great efforts in these areas. We just want to suggest that there is much that still needs to be done. Why not start this Christmas season? And right now, today!

Let us offer a prayer and light a Christ candle of hope to help us in these efforts.

CHRIST CANDLE OF HOPE PRAYER

God, our loving Father, You sent Your Son, Jesus Christ, into this world to counter all the forces of evil—sin, suffering, and death—and to overcome evil with the force of good, hatred with the power of love, Your great love for us in Jesus.

Help us never to curse the darkness, but to join with You in bringing Your light into this world, the light that is Your Son, born of the Virgin Mary, in Bethlehem.

Help us to be instruments of Your light and love by doing one special act of kindness or by being Your special instrument of reconciliation this Christmas season.

May the Christ candle we light symbolize our desire to bring light into a world of darkness and hope into a world of despair.

We ask this through Christ Our Lord. Amen.

January 8

Practicing Ecumenism with Practical Ecumenism

Most people do not have the training or background to engage in high-level ecumenical discussions with members of other religious communities. My friend Dr. Timothy George, founding dean of the Beeson Divinity School at Samford University in Birmingham, Alabama, does have the proper qualifications.

For years, Dean George participated in ecumenical dialogue between Roman Catholics and Baptists on the international level and contributed greatly to discussions that took place through the years in Rome and elsewhere.

While I was bishop of Birmingham, he and I met on occasion to discuss matters of mutual concern. We worked together to organize a broad-based conference on race relations between black and white communities in our country, which was hosted at Beeson Divinity School in March 2016. A talented group of speakers from around the world participated, including Archbishop Anthony Obinna, the archbishop of Owerri in Nigeria.

How important collaboration is with other religious communities to address critical issues of our day that call for working together with others.

Christ's call for unity among His followers (see John 17:21) is not a hollow command to be taken lightly.

Everyone can do his or her part for the cause of Christian unity in one way or another, especially in the practical ways of ecumenism.

Pope Francis exemplified the practical path to ecumenism in his apostolic journey to South Sudan in February 2023, which has been described as a "pilgrimage of companionship."

The archbishop of Canterbury and the moderator of the General Assembly of the Scottish Presbyterian Church accompanied Pope Francis on his visit to South Sudan in order to show a unified appeal of Christian leaders in addressing peace efforts in Sudan. Their collaboration worked!

The archbishop made the remark during an ecumenical prayer service on February 4 that "the only way the world will know Jesus came from the Father is when the followers are one, for God is one."

Pope Francis gave us an example to look for ways to join our brothers and sisters of other faiths to address complicated issues in our society that we cannot resolve alone. In so doing, we are practicing practical ecumenism.

Let us lift up our prayers for practical ways to bring others together with us in addressing critical issues in our backyard, as we light a candle and pray the Christ Candle of Hope Prayer.

CHRIST CANDLE OF HOPE PRAYER

God, our loving Father, You sent Your Son, Jesus Christ, into this world to counter all the forces of evil—sin, suffering, and death—and to overcome evil with the force of good, hatred with the power of love, Your great love for us in Jesus.

Help us never to curse the darkness, but to join with You in bringing Your light into this world, the light that is Your Son, born of the Virgin Mary, in Bethlehem.

Help us to be instruments of Your light and love by doing one special act of kindness or by being Your special instrument of reconciliation this Christmas season.

May the Christ candle we light symbolize our desire to bring light into a world of darkness and hope into a world of despair.

We ask this through Christ Our Lord. Amen.

January 9

The Ways of Practical Ecumenism

In early January each year, the Church urges us to celebrate a week of prayer for Christian unity. Though unity may seem understandably a far-off goal for us, we are, as followers of Jesus, bound to work and pray for the realization of that goal of Jesus in John's Gospel: "that they may all be one, as you, Father, are in me and I am in you, may they also be one in us.... So that the world may know that you have sent me" (17:21).

There are, actually, many concrete, practical ways that we can realize a measure of that unity. We just need to be creative and act.

While in charge of a university parish in Gainesville, Florida, in the late 1970s, I was confronted with people living on the street who came to our St. Augustine parish for food and shelter. Many of them came off nearby Interstate 75. The federal government had fomented much of the problem by decreasing funding for mental institutions and releasing people to the streets with medications, but no food or place to stay.

First, we handed out peanut butter sandwiches. Then, with the help of other Catholic parishes, with the support of pastors of Episcopal and Presbyterian churches in the city, and with the leadership of a very generous woman, Carmen Caudron, we launched our St. Francis soup kitchen in a garage of a former convent nearby.

We later established a shelter, which was also under the patronage of St. Francis. With the guidance of two dedicated priests—Fr. Roland Julien, pastor of St. Patrick's parish, and Fr. John Gillespie, my successor at St. Augustine's university parish, the soup kitchen and shelter were combined in one new, enormous St. Francis soup kitchen and shelter that exists today.

Later, when I became pastor of our Cathedral parish in St. Augustine, Florida, we collaborated again ecumenically with Episcopalians, Presbyterians, and others to launch another St. Francis house to serve people living on the streets of St. Augustine, many of whom came off Interstate 95. A lady by the name of Joan Lohr took the lead in this ecumenical effort.

The two St. Francis houses, in Gainesville and St. Augustine, Florida, still help the needy today, many years after their founding. No one religious community could have addressed the need alone.

I think of another grassroots ecumenical project: this one is a march for life in Birmingham held in early January each year and organized by a marvelous leader, Jim Pinto, a convert to Catholicism, and supported by Lee John Bruno and the United for Life ecumenical organization. This annual march for life is a powerful witness for life that is organized collaboratively by dedicated laypeople. Jim and his wife, Joy, also operate Her Choice, an apostolate to assist couples with unexpected pregnancies, which is another great ecumenical endeavor.

In 2020, I retired as bishop of Birmingham to a neighborhood near our Camp Tekakwitha, where I now help with Masses and talk to various groups on retreat.

A neighbor across the street from my home, Louis Wilhite, welcomed me to the neighborhood. He also is retired, and he is a Baptist minister. We have become very close friends.

After the death of his wife, I have visited him at times, once on Ash Wednesday. On that Wednesday, I made the offer to give him ashes on his forehead if he were open to that ecumenical gesture. He responded wholeheartedly to welcome this Catholic sacramental. He explained to me that he was going to a service that Wednesday evening at a Presbyterian church, joined by his relatives. So why not receive blessed ashes now?

Those Presbyterians must have greeted him with smiles when he told them who placed the ashes on his forehead!

Can you think of ways you may foster practical ecumenism in your own backyard with a spirit of unity brought about by a prayer, a gesture, or an act of kindness?

Let us offer a prayer and light a Christ candle of hope.

Christ Candle of Hope Prayer

God, our loving Father, You sent Your Son, Jesus Christ, into this world to counter all the forces of evil—sin, suffering, and death—and to overcome evil with the force of good, hatred with the power of love, Your great love for us in Jesus.

Help us never to curse the darkness, but to join with You in bringing Your light into this world, the light that is Your Son, born of the Virgin Mary, in Bethlehem.

Help us to be instruments of Your light and love by doing one special act of kindness or by being Your special instrument of reconciliation this Christmas season.

May the Christ candle we light symbolize our desire to bring light into a world of darkness and hope into a world of despair.

We ask this through Christ Our Lord. Amen.

January 10

Responding to Violence and Reducing Conflict

Pope Francis accurately described the sentiments of many people who face the threat of increasing violent activity in their towns and cities when he said that "we have such need in these times that can appear dark, in which we sometimes feel disoriented by the evil and violence that surrounds us.... We need hope.... We must not let hope abandon us, because God, with his love, walks with us."

To get from my home to Birmingham, I often drive through the town of Tarrant, where a resident has a one-in-fifty-six chance of being confronted by some violent activity, such as being attacked or murdered. In parts of the town of Fairfield near Birmingham, the odds of facing violent crime are worse. People in many cities throughout our country live in fear of the violence escalating in their communities.

How does one find hope in situations such as these?

In my experience as a priest and bishop, I have found that much violent activity is associated with addictive behavior and the proliferation of drug habits. Countering drug use should be a major effort in reducing violent crime in our culture. For the past thirty years, I have given attention to Catholic efforts to help people find alternatives to addictive behavior.

My dear friend Mother Elvira Petrozzi, an Italian consecrated religious who founded the Cenacolo community, has shown me that there is a way out of the drug culture and the violent behavior that flows from it. She now has over seventy communities throughout the world that provide support in a prayer-based, Eucharistically-centered, motivationally-oriented community that targets the problem behind the use of drugs. That problem is related to the secular culture that emphasizes selfishness, pleasure, and worldly values instead of service, sacrifice, and a relationship with God. Mother Elvira had guided people to the alternative values that orient people away from violence until her death on August 3, 2023.

More efforts in a positive direction to counter violence are needed in our society. Jesus radically and drastically calls for a unique approach to violence when He says:

> You have heard the commandment, 'an eye for an eye, a tooth for a tooth.' But what I say to you is: offer no resistance to injury. When a person strikes you on the right cheek, offer him the other: If anyone wants to go to law over your shirt, hand him your coat as well. (Matt. 5:38–40)

It is interesting that the heading over this passage of the New American Bible is "The New Law of Retaliation." Jesus' approach to violence supersedes the old approach of *lex talionis*, "an eye for an eye and a tooth for a tooth."

Of course, Jesus not only talked about this teaching but also lived this teaching and died living it out.

What we have from Jesus is a model and a goal.

The Judeo-Christian message always challenges people to conversion. Recall the words of the Lord from the prophet Ezekiel: "As I live, says the lord God, I swear I take no pleasure in the death of the wicked man, but rather in the wicked man's conversion, that he may live. Turn, turn from your evil ways!" (Ezek. 33:11).

The incarceration of criminals is necessary to prevent crime in our society. But the Christian approach is always toward rehabilitation and conversion. This reality is the basis for the Catholic Church's strong commitment to prison ministry. This approach also underlies the efforts of recent popes to seek alternatives to capital punishment.

In what way can I lend my assistance to programs helping people who are addicted to drugs? How can I help people in prisons to find their way to spiritual healing and conversion?

How can I bring hope to these situations where violence lurks, not compounding violence with violence? How can I implement Pope Francis's exhortation to "not let hope abandon us, because God, with his love, walks with us"?

Let us light a Christ candle of hope and offer a prayer.

CHRIST CANDLE OF HOPE PRAYER

God, our loving Father, You sent Your Son, Jesus Christ, into this world to counter all the forces of evil—sin, suffering, and death—and to overcome evil with the force of good, hatred with the power of love, Your great love for us in Jesus.

Help us never to curse the darkness, but to join with You in bringing Your light into this world, the light that is Your Son, born of the Virgin Mary, in Bethlehem.

Help us to be instruments of Your light and love by doing one special act of kindness or by being Your special instrument of reconciliation this Christmas season.

May the Christ candle we light symbolize our desire to bring light into a world of darkness and hope into a world of despair.

We ask this through Christ Our Lord. Amen.

January 11

The Holy Eucharist, Our Hope and Our Joy

According to a 2015 Pew research study, around 39 percent of American Catholics attend Mass each Sunday. Only 4 percent of those termed "cultural Catholics" do so. These percentages have changed since the COVID-19 scare resulted in the closing of churches. Church attendance has dropped significantly and has not returned to pre-COVID numbers.

If it's any consolation, though it shouldn't be, the percentage of weekly Mass attendance in Europe is far worse. In the Netherlands, only 7 percent of self-identified Catholics attend Mass weekly. Cardinal Wilhelm Eijk, primate of the Netherlands and president of the Dutch bishops' conference, says that "Christ has become a virtually unknown figure to most Dutch people today."[40]

The American bishops have long known they have a problem on their hands, and they are rallying efforts to re-catechize their congregations on the nature and importance of the Holy Eucharist.

---

[40] *National Catholic Register*, February 12, 2023, p. 4.

I have found the saints to be great models for us bishops in this critical effort, and one young recently beatified Italian in particular: Blessed Carlo Acutis.

Blessed Carlo was beatified on October 10, 2020, in Assisi, the town in which his mortal remains are interred, in the old cathedral of Santa Maria Maggiore, also referred to as the *Sanctuario della Spolliazione*, where St. Francis divested himself of all his possessions.

Blessed Carlo lived just short of fifteen years, from 1991 to 2006. Since his death in 2006, he has captured the attention of many thousands of young people in Europe and around the world as a model of faith. I recommend the short biography by Monsignor Anthony Figueiredo, S.T.D., *Blessed Carlo Acutis: 5 Steps to Being a Saint* for a good introduction to his life.[41]

Carlo is noted for beautiful insights into the Christian life, such as: "To be always close to Jesus—that's my life plan.... Our aim has to be the infinite and not the finite.... The infinite is our homeland. We have always been expected in heaven."

"Everyone is born as an original, but many people end up dying as photocopies." "The more we receive the Eucharist, the more we will become like Jesus, so that on this earth we will have a foretaste of heaven.... The Eucharist is truly the heart of Jesus.... Try to go to Mass every day and to receive holy communion.... You go straight to heaven if you participate in the mass every day."

And Blessed Carlo called the Eucharist his "highway to heaven." As a teenager, adept at using a computer, he established a website of Eucharistic miracles and managed to send, with his parents' help, displays of miracles associated with the Eucharist to parishes around the world.

---

[41] Anthony Figueiredo, *Blessed Carlo Acutis: 5 Steps to Being a Saint* (London: Catholic Truth Society, 2021).

Blessed Carlo's special devotion to the Eucharist began when he received his first Holy Communion. He had a unique insight, perhaps an infused grace from God, that this was Jesus truly, really, and substantially present. He came to see that if one truly believed that this is really Jesus present in the Eucharist, one would naturally want to be with Him often. Consequently, Blessed Carlo attended Mass daily until shortly before his death. As his mother, Antonia, humbly points out, it was not her example that led him to his Eucharistic devotion, because she herself had stopped attending Mass. It was blessed Carlo who brought her back to faithful attendance at holy Mass.

In early October of 2006, Carlo became sick and was thought to have had the flu, but he was diagnosed with an aggressive form of leukemia. A short time later, on October 12, Carlo's life began to slip away. He died that day with amazing courage and deep faith.

Permission was granted to him to be buried in Assisi because of his great devotion to St. Francis and also because of his generous volunteer service in the area of Assisi.

Blessed Carlo is a modern-day evangelist of the Holy Eucharist, especially to young people. We pray that many people, especially of the millennial generation of which Blessed Carlo Acutis was a member, may find their way back to the Lord of the Eucharist through his powerful intercession.

Let us light a Christ candle of hope for that intention.

CHRIST CANDLE OF HOPE PRAYER

God, our loving Father, You sent Your Son, Jesus Christ, into this world to counter all the forces of evil—sin, suffering, and death—and to overcome evil with the force of good, hatred with the power of love, Your great love for us in Jesus.

Help us never to curse the darkness, but to join with You in bringing Your light into this world, the light that is Your Son, born of the Virgin Mary, in Bethlehem.

Help us to be instruments of Your light and love by doing one special act of kindness or by being Your special instrument of reconciliation this Christmas season.

May the Christ candle we light symbolize our desire to bring light into a world of darkness and hope into a world of despair.

We ask this through Christ Our Lord. Amen.

January 12

Connecting Joy with Hope

In a letter to the philosopher Jacques Maritain, the French Catholic author Leon Bloy (1846–1917) wrote that "joy is the infallible sign of the presence of God."

We also know from St. Paul that joy is one of the fruits of the Holy Spirit's activity (see Gal. 5:22) and that against the fruits of the Spirit there is no law (see v. 23). Those fruits are uniquely derived by the Spirit's activity. So Leon Bloy is right. If joy is present, God is in some way present. Only God can bring about true joy.

The theme of joy runs throughout the Old and New Testaments and is often associated with God's presence and activity. The angel Gabriel tells Mary there is a reason for rejoicing: "Rejoice, O highly favored daughter! The lord is with you. Blessed are you among women" (Luke 1:28). An angel appears to shepherds keeping night watch over their flocks and proclaims good news to them: "Tidings of great joy to be shared by the whole people. This day in David's city a Savior has been born to you, the Messiah and Lord. Let this be a sign to you: in a manger you will find an infant wrapped in swaddling clothes" (Luke 2:10–12).

In all of salvation history, the ultimate joy is brought about by the birth of the Messiah. The long-awaited hope of Israel is realized in the birth of Jesus of Nazareth, the Son of God. Hope and joy connect in the birth of Jesus Christ. God being with us in Jesus, Emmanuel, is a true joy and the realization of all our human hopes and joys. In Him is all our hope. In Him is all our joy. Everything else is partial, incomplete, or temporary joy.

St. Paul connects joy and hope in his letter to the Romans: "Rejoice in hope, be patient under trial, persevere in prayer" (12:12).

St. Thomas Aquinas describes joy (*gaudium*) as springing from the "knowledge or the performance of a good, the actual possession and enjoyment of good." According to St. Thomas, there can be a *gaudium rei*, the joy that springs from a good held in possession according to reality, or a *gaudium spei*, the joy that springs from the hope for the possession of this good.[42]

Hope gives us joy as we embrace a deep longing for something or someone special. The simple expectation is a cause for joy. We know that we do not yet possess what we long for or whom we long for. It is a good that is realizable, yet not yet fully possessed.

In the virtue of hope, we have the seeds of joy. There is an expectation in the hope of a reality that we know is coming. There is an expectation of that reality arriving; there is great anticipation. There is indeed a taste of joy because of hope itself.

Our reason for hope and joy was the birth of the Messiah. Our cause of hope and joy in the face of all the dilemmas, disappointments, disruptions, disillusionment, and desperations of everyday life is the enduring presence of God in our lives here and now—today—especially in the Sacraments, especially in the Holy Eucharist. God is Emmanuel! God is with us in Jesus. And Jesus is really, truly, and substantially with us in the most Holy Eucharist.

---

[42] *A Latin-English Dictionary of St. Thomas Aquinas*, ed. Roy J. Defferrari (Boston: St. Paul Editions, 1960), 429.

God is not a distant God. In every situation, and every instance of everyday life, God is with us. We only need to acknowledge His presence with a prayer, anytime, anywhere!

In this Christmas season, may we truly rejoice in hope as we light a candle and pray the special Christ Candle of Hope Prayer.

CHRIST CANDLE OF HOPE PRAYER

God, our loving Father, You sent Your Son, Jesus Christ, into this world to counter all the forces of evil—sin, suffering, and death—and to overcome evil with the force of good, hatred with the power of love, Your great love for us in Jesus.

Help us never to curse the darkness, but to join with You in bringing Your light into this world, the light that is Your Son, born of the Virgin Mary, in Bethlehem.

Help us to be instruments of Your light and love by doing one special act of kindness or by being Your special instrument of reconciliation this Christmas season.

May the Christ candle we light symbolize our desire to bring light into a world of darkness and hope into a world of despair.

We ask this through Christ Our Lord. Amen.

Baptism of the Lord (A Movable Feast)

Living Hope and Joy through Our Baptism

In a sermon about Jesus' Baptism in the Jordan by John, St. Maximus of Turin (380–c. 465), the first known bishop of Turin, asks, "Why would a holy man desire Baptism?" And he poses this answer: "Christ is baptized, not to be made holy by the water, but to make the water holy.... When the Savior is washed all water for our baptism is made clean, purified at its source for the dispensing of baptismal grace to the people of future ages. Christ is the first to be baptized, then, so that Christians will follow after him with confidence."[43]

Christ enters into the ritual baptism of John to inaugurate Baptism as the sacramental means of grace for us. Before leaving this world, He gave His eleven disciples the great commission to "go ... and make disciples of all the nations. Baptize them in the name of the Father, and of the Son, and of the Holy Spirit. Teach them to carry out everything I have commanded you. And know that I am with you always, until the end of the world" (Matt. 28:19–20).

---

[43] *The Liturgy of the Hours*, vol. 1 (New York: Catholic Book Publishing, 1975), 612, 613.

Pope Francis, speaking of this mandate for all the baptized to bring the Gospel message to the world, says:

> In all the baptized, from first to last, the sanctifying power of the Spirit is at work, impelling us to evangelization....
>
> In virtue of their baptism, all the members of the People of God have become missionary disciples (cf. Mt. 28:19). All the baptized, whatever their position in the Church or their level of instruction in the faith, are agents of evangelization, and it would be insufficient to envisage a plan of evangelization to be carried out by professionals while the rest of the faithful would simply be passive recipients. The new evangelization calls for personal involvement on the part of each of the baptized. Every Christian is challenged, here and now, to be actively engaged in evangelization; indeed, anyone who has truly experienced God's saving love does not need much time or lengthy training to go out and proclaim that love. Every Christian is a missionary to the extent that he or she has encountered the love of God in Christ Jesus; we no longer say that we are "disciples" and "missionaries," but rather that we are always "missionary disciples."[44]

Here, Pope Francis gives us his marching orders and makes it clear that no Catholic should feel comfortable sitting back and doing nothing. Previous popes in recent years have suggested the same. Pope St. John Paul II called for a New Evangelization in a 1983 address to bishops of Latin America, where he said that this New Evangelization was not new in content but in ardor,

---

[44] Francis, Apostolic Exhortation *Evangelii Gaudium* (November 24, 2013), nos. 119, 120.

methods, and expression.[45] In *Redemptoris Missio*, he wrote that "faith is strengthened when it is given to others."[46]

The mandate of the Spirit through the Sacrament of Baptism to evangelize becomes greater with the Sacrament of Confirmation, where confirmed Catholics receive a call within the original baptismal call. It is a call to a more particular form of evangelizing, whether in the single life, the married life, the consecrated religious life, or the priesthood. Even within those states of life, the Holy Spirit summons people through the grace of Confirmation to particular areas of evangelization, reflecting the individual's gifts and talents.

What is the mission the Holy Spirit is leading me to here and now, today? How am I fulfilling the grace to evangelize, which comes from the Sacraments of Baptism and Confirmation? How am I reflecting the joy I have received in my encounter with Jesus?

"The joy of the Gospel fills the hearts and lives of all who encounter Jesus. Those who accept his offer of salvation are set free from sin, sorrow, inner emptiness and loneliness. With Christ joy is constantly born anew."[47]

Let us pray a prayer and light a Christ candle of hope in gratitude for the gift of our Baptism and Confirmation, which give us great joy and empower us to be missionary disciples of Jesus Christ, bringing hope and joy to all we are called to serve.

[45] John Paul II, Address to CELAM (March 9, 1983).
[46] John Paul II, Encyclical Letter *Redemptoris Missio* (December 7, 1990), no. 2.
[47] Francis, *Evangelii Gaudium*, no. 1.

REJOICING IN OUR HOPE

CHRIST CANDLE OF HOPE PRAYER

God, our loving Father, You sent Your Son, Jesus Christ, into this world to counter all the forces of evil—sin, suffering, and death—and to overcome evil with the force of good, hatred with the power of love, Your great love for us in Jesus.

Help us never to curse the darkness, but to join with You in bringing Your light into this world, the light that is Your Son, born of the Virgin Mary, in Bethlehem.

Help us to be instruments of Your light and love by doing one special act of kindness or by being Your special instrument of reconciliation this Christmas season.

May the Christ candle we light symbolize our desire to bring light into a world of darkness and hope into a world of despair.

We ask this through Christ Our Lord. Amen.

February 2

Feast of the Presentation of the Lord, "Candlemas Day"

Recent popes have left the crib in St. Peter's piazza up until February 2, which is the fortieth day after Christmas. You might wish to follow their example. Each year, the rendition of the birth of Christ at the Vatican takes on a different character, creatively representing different cultures or different designs to bring home each year the beauty of the mystery of the birth of Jesus Christ.

I display my personal Christmas crib in my private chapel in my home all through the year. I purchased wood-carved images of the Christmas story in Rome, Italy, over several years while a student there in the early 1970s. They were designed by a man named Ferràndiz for the Anri company and are very impressive.

Mother Angelica had an exhibition of the Christmas crib built in a cave-like structure on the grounds of her monastery in Hanceville, Alabama, which she left on display all year long. Near Assisi, Italy, in the valley, a rendition of the Christmas crib is displayed near the basilica of Santa Maria deli Angeli all year long, as it was St. Francis who initiated that devotion with a live nativity.

It was the prophetess Anna, along with Simeon, who greeted Mary and Joseph on the day when they presented Jesus in the

Temple in Jerusalem, observing Jewish custom to present a first-born child in the Temple and for the mother to be purified after giving birth.

Like Simeon, Anna recognized this child as someone special and "spoke about the child to all who were awaiting the redemption of Jerusalem" (Luke 2:38).

It is our great privilege to do as Anna the prophetess did, to be evangelizers of the presence and activity of Jesus, Who was born in Bethlehem to Mary and Joseph! We are disciples of Jesus Christ and missionaries for Him to the world, to the very ends of the earth. Whatever the situation, wherever the place, we are called to bring the light of Christ into the darkness of the world that surrounds us, and to do so in hope and joy.

No problem is too great that it cannot be overcome by the blessing of Jesus Christ. His birth overcame the darkness and enables us to walk confidently through every form of darkness—sin, suffering, and death—to enter into the light that is Christ. We are called to be instruments of overturning darkness with light, the bright light that is Jesus Christ!

Proclaim the light that is Christ! Live that light that is Christ! Confront every form of darkness with the light that is Christ!

By your Baptism and the Sacrament of Confirmation, you were given the light of Christ. At Baptism and the Easter Vigil ceremony, you held a candle symbolizing the light of Christ and your role as a missionary disciple of Christ to bring light into the world. Boldly and confidently, with joyful hope, carry light into the world, the light that Jesus brought into this world at His birth! He is with you in every moment of your life, as you bring His light and enable Him to be reborn into the lives of all those you bring to Him by the power of His light, His life, and His love!

Feast of the Presentation of the Lord, "Candlemas Day"

CHRIST CANDLE OF HOPE PRAYER

God, our loving Father, You sent Your Son, Jesus Christ, into this world to counter all the forces of evil—sin, suffering, and death—and to overcome evil with the force of good, hatred with the power of love, Your great love for us in Jesus.

Help us never to curse the darkness, but to join with You in bringing Your light into this world, the light that is Your Son, born of the Virgin Mary, in Bethlehem.

Help us to be instruments of Your light and love by doing one special act of kindness or by being Your special instrument of reconciliation this Christmas season.

May the Christ candle we light symbolize our desire to bring light into a world of darkness and hope into a world of despair.

We ask this through Christ Our Lord. Amen.

Spe Gaudentes: Rejoicing in Hope

Our joy is in hope.
—Romans: 12:12

Where is joy to be found?
Is it in good health? Success? Friends and family?
As we grow spiritually, we come to understand that
true joy can't be tied to the present moment. As wonderful as those moments might seem, every one of
them can be taken away in an instant, and when that
happens, where will our happiness be rooted?

But if our joy is in hope, then our joy is connected,
not to what we have, but to what we will have. If our
guiding principle lies in looking forward to the eternal
happiness to come, then joy can never be lost....

It's a calm realization that what lies ahead exceeds even
the greatest joy we can feel in any of our earthly moments. Let

your joy be in hope. This can be one of our greatest blessings and a true directive for the identity of a real Christian.[48]

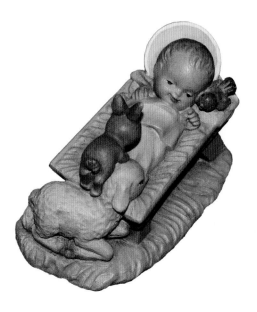

[48] Lambert Reilly, *Latin Sayings for Spiritual Growth* (Huntington, IN: Our Sunday Visitor Press, 2001), 74–75.

References and Resources

Acutis, Antonia Salzano, with Paolo Rosario. *My Son, Carlo: Carlo Acutis through the Eyes of His Mother.* Huntington, IN: Our Sunday Visitor Press, 2023.

Baker, Robert J. *Called, Formed, Sent (Llamados, Formados, Enviados): Pastoral Letter on Missionary Discipleship and Its Consequences for Ministry in the Diocese of Birmingham.* Birmingham, AL: One Voice Press, 2018.

———. *Prayers of Desperation: A Questioner's Prayer for Answers in Our Darkest Moments.* Irondale, AL: EWTN Publishing, Inc.

———. *The Redemption of Our Bodies: The Theology of the Body and Its Consequences for Ministry in the Diocese of Charleston.* Charleston, SC: Miscellany Press, Diocese of Charleston, 2005.

Baker, Robert J., with Timothy George and William A. Bell. *Black and White in America: How Deep the Divide? Text of Conference Talks and Panel Discussions.* Edited by Amy Welborn and Revised by Frances Smith. Diocese of Birmingham Office of Black Catholics Publication, 2021.

Baker, Robert J., with Benedict Groeschel. *When Did We See You, Lord?* Huntington, IN: Our Sunday Visitor Press, 2005.

Benedict XVI (pope). Encyclical Letter *Spe Salvi.* November 30, 2007.

Catoir, John T. *Enjoy the Lord: A Path to Contemplation.* New York, NY: Arena Lettres, 1978.

Delp, Alfred. *Advent of the Heart: Seasonal Sermons and Prison Writings, 1941–1944*. San Francisco: Ignatius Press, 2006.

Figueiredo, Anthony. *Blessed Carlo Acutis: 5 Steps to Being a Saint*. London: Catholic Truth Society, 2021.

Flannery, Austin. *Vatican Council II*. Vol. 1, *The Conciliar and Postconciliar Documents*. New Revised Edition. Dublin, Ireland: Dominican Publications, Third Printing, 1996.

Francis (pope). Apostolic Exhortation *Evangelii Gaudium*. November 24, 2013.

———. *On Hope*. Chicago: Loyola Press, 2017.

———. "The Whole World Is at War, We Must Stop!: In-Flight Press Conference with the Archbishop of Canterbury and the Moderator of the General Assembly of the Church of Scotland." *L'Osservatore Romano*, English Edition, February 10, 2023, no. 6, pp. 12–15.

Gratton, Carolyn. *Trusting: Theory and Practice*. New York: Crossroad Publishing, 1982.

Groeschel, Benedict. *After This Life: What Catholics Believe about What Happens Next*. Huntington, IN: Our Sunday Visitor Press, 2009.

John Paul II (pope). Encyclical Letter *Dives in Misericordia*. November 30, 1980.

Kowalska, Maria Faustina. *Diary of Saint Maria Faustina Kowalska: Divine Mercy in My Soul*. Stockbridge, MA: Marian Press, 2005.

Martin, George, ed. *Hope. A Publication by God's Word Today, A Daily Guide to Reading Scripture*. Ann Arbor, MI: Servant Publications. December, 1987.

New American Bible. New York: Catholic Book Publishing, 1970.

Petrozzi, Elvira. *The Embrace of God's Mercy: Mother Elvira and the Story of Community Cenacolo*. Manchester, NH: Sophia Institiute Press, 2019.

Weaver, Bertrand. *Joy*. New York: Sheed & Ward, 1964.

About the Author

Bishop Robert J. Baker, S.T.D., served as bishop of Charleston, South Carolina, from 1999 to 2007 and as bishop of Birmingham, Alabama, from 2007 to 2020. He has published numerous articles and books, including *Prayers of Desperation* and *When Did We See You, Lord?*, which he co-authored with Father Benedict J. Groeschel, C.F.R.